Contents

Foreword   5
What is newsreel?   *Lisa Pontecorvo*   6
Abstracts   8
Newsreel organisations   84
Newsreel staff   *Lisa Pontecorvo*   86
Newsreel libraries and archives   96
Documentation centres   106

Appendices
1   Examples of typical issue sheets   110
2   Some early catalogues of topical films held by the National Film Archive
        Cataloguing Department   112
3   Films and videos about the British newsreels   113

[Chronological chart—separate insert]

Subject index to Abstracts   116

VISIT THE
L·N·E·R—PATHE
MOBILE NEWS CINEMA
attached to this Train

PROGRAMME

Commencing 28th November, 1936

TIMES OF SHOWING

From KING'S CROSS	To KING'S CROSS
10.35 a.m.	3.20 p.m.
11.55 a.m.	4.25 p.m.
1.05 p.m.	5.45 p.m.

PATHE GAZETTE

THE KING IN SOUTH WALES.
THE PRIME MINISTER SPEAKS TO THE NATION.
100 to 1 WINNER WOTAN WINS MELBOURNE CUP IN RECORD TIME.
FOREST FIRE IN NORTH WEST PACIFIC TOWN OF OREGON.
COUNT CIANO IN AUSTRIA.
INTERNATIONAL FOOTBALL IN RUSSIA.
RUSSIAN PROVISIONS FOR SPAIN.
U.S. TUG-O'-WAR IN THE MUD.
AMERICA REMEMBERS GREAT WAR DEAD.
EXPLOSION IN AMMUNITION FACTORY NEAR MARSEILLES.
U.S. LIVESTOCK AND POULTRY SHOWS.
MARATHON WALKING RACE IN NEW YORK STATE.
WORLD'S WONDER BRIDGE OPENED.
FRENCH CABINET MINISTER'S FUNERAL.
MILLION TON BLAST.
YORKSHIRE MOTOR CYCLE TRIAL.
POLICE USE SMOKE BOMBS.

PATHETONE WEEKLY

TUNA—FISHING FOR TUNA, OR TUNNY, IN WATERS OF NEW
    JERSEY.
DINNER IS SERVED—THE CHIMP FAMILY.
CINEVIEWS IN BRIEF—CAUGHT BY THE CAMERA.
FAMOUS FOOTBALL TEAMS AT HOME—NO. 1. "BRENTFORD."
JACK HART AND HIS BAND—CELEBRATED ORCHESTRA.

PATHE PICTORIAL

LOOK WHO'S HERE—WHO'S KNOCKING AT THE DOOR.
TWO OLD SALTS—WHO KNIT JERSEYS WHEN NOT MENDING NETS.
SAFETY FIRST—CHILD'S MACKINTOSHES.
ARTHUR WILLIAMS—TENOR SINGING "THE ROSE OF TRALEE."
HUNTING DRAGONS—MALAY ARCHIPELAGO.
RONALD FRANKAU—COMEDIAN BROADCASTER WITH MONTY
    CRICK AT THE PIANO.

THE KING

ADMISSION - 1/-
(Including Tax)

Printed in Great Britain by Knapp, Drewett & Sons Ltd., London and Kingston-on-Thames   20037R.   2.500

(Reproduced by kind permission of Thorn-EMI Pathé and BFI Library Services)

Foreword

It was generally agreed by reviewers that the *Researcher's Guide to British Film & Television Collections*, published by the then British Universities Film Council in 1981, filled a gap in the literature of film and television. That publication was based on the pioneering work of the staff of the Slade Film History Register. The *Researcher's Guide to British Newsreels* is a companion volume. The British Universities Film & Video Council, through its experience in administering the Register, came to recognise the need for a document that would illustrate the history and development of the newsreels and cinemagazines, point to the considerable amount of research that has been done in recent years and at the same time serve as a practical reference work for film and television researchers. Clearly the compilation of this Guide also owes a debt to those historians who have written about the newsreels.

Unlike its predecessor, which will be updated as need arises, this Guide is not expected to run to a second edition. That is not to say that we think the contents will not need updating. There are almost certainly some articles that we should have abstracted but have missed and there will possibly be some revisions that should be made to the lists of newsreel staff who worked up to and including the Second World War. On both scores we should very much welcome any information that would correct, improve, or update the contents.

A chronological chart showing the period covered by the newsreels has been devised as a quick visual reference and is enclosed with this Guide.

The main purpose of the Guide is to serve as a reference document for the working researcher but we hope that those engaged in media studies may also find it useful.

What is newsreel?

Lisa Pontecorvo

Newsreel differs from documentary film and from the early actualities, or 'topicals' that filled out the programmes of film shows until 1908, when the French company Pathé first assembled the 'topicals' into regular issues. Newsreel takes a short term view based on the expectations of a mass audience. It was an assemblage of various events and topics, issued regularly, once or twice weekly, and had to be an agreed unvariable length to fit into the cinema show before the feature film. The newsreel developed from show business rather than journalism, and had international rather than national roots from the start. There are certain features that are common to cinema newsreels in every country at most periods of their development from 1908. But it is wrong to think of newsreels as something monolithic and unchanging over the seventy odd years of their existence, as even the five main British newsreel companies varied in their style and practice.

There was a flourishing actuality scene in Britain well before the era of newsreel proper. As part of the entertainment, one reel news events were shown in music halls on the same night as they were filmed. But the rise of the newsreel followed the commercial development of the feature film industry in France before 1914. It coincided with the changeover to permanent, purpose-built cinemas from 1908, and the growth in film distribution whereby film prints were rented rather than sold outright. Film-making then became distinct from film distribution. The early link between featurettes and actuality that had characterised the earliest film shows of Lumière actualities and Méliès fantasies continued in the public cinema show. Commercial feature film producers like Pathé and Gaumont, both French companies, subsidised newsreel production as a prestige activity to keep their name on the screen and keep a rival's name off it. Before 1914 London, Berlin and Moscow received a French newsreel version of their own news. Few countries at that time had a film industry of a size able to cope with the demands of newsreel production.

It is expensive to provide a regular national coverage: to commission local cameramen or send your staff cameramen round the country and abroad. Technology is necessary to provide camera and projection equipment; raw filmstock and processing laboratories, which all cost money. The newsreel depended on speedy transport, as well as on a network of cinemas to show it. This bound it to a supranational organisation for its development and it is within this context that we must place the British newsreel. Until the coming of sound on film in the late 1920s the European newsreel, particularly that of the French companies, was dominant. With the large capital investment and expertise involved in the changeover to sound equipment US capital and enterprise began to dominate. So in Britain the new Movietone and Paramount newsreels were produced by the American-financed feature film companies of 20th Century Fox and Paramount, but the earliest had been the French Pathé and Gaumont. *Topical Budget*, the first purely British newsreel, was not issued until 1911.

The coming of sound had the further effect of making newsreels more dependent on a local format that would appeal to their own countries' audience. So whilst Movietone offices in America might exchange material with British Movietone, the format of both their newsreel issues would be quite different because the reel was now an artefact of picture and sound, and neither English version could be shown in Paris for example, without considerable changes to accommodate the French language. This was equally true of Pathé and Gaumont French editions, which could not be freely issued in London merely by substituting a translation of the subtitles of a silent film version and keeping the same assemblage.

Nowadays people have regular television viewing habits; their expectations are known, and they watch TV news between programmes primarily designed for entertainment. The same was true of the cinema audiences who saw the regular newsreel. The pairing of a particular fiction film with certain newsreels was purely haphazard but the emotional experience for the spectator would make each the reflection of the other. The appeal of the newsreel was not that of 'hot news': the results of the Derby or football match would already be known to the audience. The appeal was that of a relived communal experience whether it was sport or a national achievement such as winning the blue riband for the fastest transatlantic crossing by the 'Queen Mary'. Unpleasant foreign news served to make home seem safer. Newsreels had the same dramatic and story-telling conventions, be they 'bad comedy', adventure, war, spectacle or human interest, as the fiction films which they accompanied.

The drama of newsreel mens' lives and the extraordinary lengths to which the newsreel company went to get back the first—perhaps the only pictures of some major event—flattered the cinema audience. Even to see the picture of some local event added to the national newsreel the day it happened was exciting, and Provincial Cinematograph Theatres had their own dark rooms attached to film projection booths so that they could do this. The 'scoops' sold the newsreel company's name to the public as did the special events like the 1911 Delhi Durbar or the 1930 coronation of Haile Selassie. Splendid imperial spectacle was brought to them by special arrangement and the fairytale magic of the East was as much an attraction as the feature film.

In 1936 it was calculated that only about 20% of the items in the newsreel were open to free editorial choice as about 40% of the issue was earmarked for sport, 20% was allocated for home news that was known ahead of time, and another 20% was given over to foreign news. So there was a strong element of prefabricated reality in newsreels by which the format overrode the news content.

How was this format arrived at? The 4–5 staff cameramen were not trained journalists and would send in their 20 weekly stories with background 'dope' sheets from which the Editor would select perhaps 8 or 9 for the final issue. It would seem that an average newsreel edition of about 9 stories was selected from some 60–90 stories. In an interview with me in 1977, H. W. Bishop corroborated this. He was a Gaumont Graphic cameraman from 1910 and later Production Manager of *Gaumont-British News*. About 20–30 stories were sent in by the locally-based Gaumont cameramen and a similar number were filmed by the 6 London-based cameramen. A further 20–30 stories were received from foreign agencies.

Technical factors such as the length of film spools also governed the shape of the newsreel. The earliest newsreels in 1910 ran for about 5 minutes, butt ending three to four items together with titling. By 1926 the super newsreels distributed to first run cinemas were double the length with a running time of about twelve to thirteen minutes, and contained twelve different items. With the coming of sound, newsreel items became longer or were bunched together as short flashes under headings like 'Sport' or 'Persons in the News'. The possibilities of commentary were exploited, and there was much discussion about how best to integrate picture and sound by using natural sound, interviews, music, sound effects and commentary.

Obviously the Editor of the newsreel was a key figure in deciding both what should be filmed and how much of that should be used in the final selection. H. W. Bishop told me in 1977 that cameramen were allocated film on a 3:1 ratio to film each story of unscripted events. This is very economical and was designed to speed editing, as it enforced a form of pre-scripting. Norman Roper of Paramount confirmed in 1977 that 4:1 was the normal British practice for newsreel filming.

It was the edited format which gave the newsreel a theme to slide in effortlessly with the feature film. The subjects the Editor chose might well mirror those highlighted in the Press, but they were chosen for majority appeal and had to conform to the norms of the British Board of Film Censors: to be suitable for showing with family films. Too much controversy might empty the cinema seats. The newsreel men captured the 'magic presence of now' for their audiences, and it has survived for us today. The relationship between the cameraman and the editor is fundamental to the newsreel and the abstracts which follow reflect the continuing debate on the structure and images of the newsreel.

Lisa Pontecorvo has a long-standing research interest in the history of newsreel. After studying history did postgraduate research on the use of film as an historical document at the Slade Film Department. For many years worked for BBC/ OU Productions, including the War and Society *series. Later worked with young children teaching them media techniques. Now working as a freelance film researcher.*

The Abstracts

Introduction

The aim of these abstracts is to illustrate the genesis, development and eventual demise of the British newsreels in particular, and the British cinemagazines incidentally, often in the words of the newsreel makers themselves and of those who have written about the reels. The essential newsreel period covered dates from *c.*1910 to the mid 1950s. The abstracts are listed under year in the following order: 1. Books, pamphlets, reports or letters; 2. Periodical articles (season, followed by month, followed by date). A chronological arrangement has been chosen because this highlights more successfully the various problems that the newsreels had to contend with at different times of their existence until the advent of television finally closed them down. Two reels survived into the seventies, *Pathé News* and *British Movietone News*, but in their latter years these increasingly assumed the character of cinemagazines.

As well as serious articles, I have listed popular comment and brief trade notices as all help to build up an overall picture of how the newsreel companies operated and how the reels were and are regarded. The bibliography is not exhaustive as there was a limit to the amount of time I could devote to the subject: I have only dipped into *The Bioscope*, for example, I have not included all *Kinematograph Weekly* references and there was no possibility of my combing through the daily and weekly newspapers. However, I have tried to include the essential items. Those contemplating further research are urged to use the facilities of the British Film Institute Library Services.

After reading many of the original articles it appeared to me that the abstracts would illuminate the newsreel era more successfully if I could quote directly on occasion rather than summarise in my own words. I have also quoted a number of short items in full. For permission to do this the BUFVC is extremely grateful to the following: Peter Noble, editor of *Screen International* (incorporating *The Cinema/To-day's Cinema* and *Kinematograph Weekly*); Penelope Houston, editor of *Sight & Sound*; Roger Manvell, original editor, *The Penguin Film Review*; Peter Avis, journal editor, *Film & Television Technician*; J. S. Skidmore, editor, *Journal of the Royal Society of Arts*; Heather Taylor, editor, *Aslib Proceedings*; BBC Publications; the Editor, *The Architect's Journal*; the Editor, *Movie Maker*; the Editor, *The Guardian*; the Editor, *New Statesman*; the Editor, *The Spectator*; the Editor, *Tribune*; Carolyn Rowlinson, John Grierson Archive; Pam Turner, Visnews; Edgar Anstey, Taylor Downing and Jim Sanger. In the few other cases where direct quotation has been employed, I have tried to trace the relevant copyright holders and apologise if, inadvertently, I have quoted without permission.

J.B.

ADDENDUM

11a   ANON. 'Empire News Bulletin'. *The Bioscope*, (20 May 1926), p. 43

Welcomes 'a new British topical containing a minimum of 350 feet of news pictures and many varied features', suitable 'for any house'. Gives production details. Goes on: 'Produced by W. C. Jeapes, and edited by Gilbert Frankau, this new British topical is a creditable piece of work both in the selection of subject matter and in the photography'. Will include 'such features as a Fashion Section for women in colours and an illustrated joke. Exclusive rights of illustrating J. L. Baird's Television process have been secured for the Bulletin and, later on, examples will be given of a new process of stereoscopic cinematography invented by Mr Jeapes. In the first issue of the Bulletin (released on May 3rd) were included excellent shots of Sir Joseph Cook visiting H.M.S. Melbourne; . . . May Day at Knutsford, Cheshire; Labour Day in London . . . and J. L. Baird's Television apparatus. The fourth issue (released on May 13th) dealt largely with scenes of the General Strike, including interesting views of volunteer stevedores working at the docks, the enrolment of special constables and the great food convoy driving through London'.

1901

1 DICKSON, W. K.-L. *The Biograph in battle: its story in the South African War related with personal experiences.* London: T. Fisher Unwin, 1901. xx, 296p.

The author, who 'had the good fortune to obtain unique privileges and permits from the military authorities,' describes his newsreel expedition to cover the Boer War during the period October 1899–June 1900.

1912

2 TALBOT, Frederick A. *Moving pictures: how they are made and worked.* London: Heinemann, 1912. xvi, 340p.

Chapter 25, 'The "animated" newspaper,' p.277–86, deals with the 'topical picture'. 'Although the animated newspaper has been amongst us for only a few months, yet it has already developed into an institution . . . The work (of producing the topical film) can be handled successfully only by a firm having an extensive organisation . . . There must be an editor to direct operations and to prepare the film. It must possess a large and scattered staff, so that no part of the world is left uncovered by a cinematograph . . . In the offices a number of skilled operators must be ready to hurry off at a moment's notice to any desired spot'. The author then goes 'behind the scenes of one of the most flourishing and successful of these animated news-sheets—*The Gaumont Graphic*' and follows it through its successive phases of production. When this reel was published weekly, at an average length of 600 feet, its circulation approximated 200 copies per week. 'Now, it is published twice weekly, and with increased success' . . . and, it 'is quite ready to appear daily if the demand should arise'.

1916

3 ANON. 'Makers of the Somme film'. *The Times* (5 September 1916), p.6.

Reports that some of the chief officials of the War Office, the Ministry of Munitions and the Board of Inventions had a private view the previous day at the Scala Theatre of the official film, "The Battle of the Somme". The demand on the part of the public to see the film is greater than ever. 'It has now been booked to more than 1,000 picture theatres throughout the kingdom'. In a letter to *The Times* the previous day Sir Arthur Conan Doyle had expressed the opinion that 'the name and portrait of the brave operator who risked his life to secure this valuable national possession should be flashed upon the screen'. The film was shot by two operators, J. B. McDowell, Managing Director of the British and Colonial Kinematograph Company, and G. H. Malins, an operator in the service of the Gaumont Company (who is responsible for about one third of the material). 'Both operators . . . are appointed by the British Topical Committee, and paid by them at the rate of £1 per day, the War Office providing travelling, transport and billet'.

1917

4 ADVERTISEMENT. *The Bioscope*, vol. 35, no. 554 (24 May 1917), p.788–9.

Two-page advertisement for the *Official War Office Topical Budget*: the British animated news-film. Text reads: 'On and after May 28th, 1917 the *Topical Budget* will be run and controlled by The War Office Cinematograph Committe. It will contain a series of *authentic* and *official* pictures dealing with the war at home and abroad. Branch offices will be arranged at an early date throughout the provinces. Book the *Topical Budget*'.

5   ANON. 'Gossip and opinions by "Projector"'. *The Bioscope*, vol. 37, no. 572 (27 September 1917), p.5–7.

On page 6 a brief item notes the acquisition by the War Office Cinematograph Committee of 'the premises, plant and staff of the Topical Film Co., Wardour Street, for the purpose of issuing twice weekly a topical war film budget illustrating the progress of events and the chief activities more or less associated with it. This step, which is distinctly one in the right direction, has been necessitated by the enormous wealth of material which is arriving daily from the various fronts, and should do much to remedy the too-frequent complaints about the scanty information given to the public. A well-defined and organised system of distribution of the films has been arranged, special care being taken to ensure their reaching all parts of the world associated with our country in the prosecution of the struggle. In this way public opinion on the side of the Allies should be considerably influenced'.

1918

6   ANON. 'Trade notes and news' *The Bioscope*, vol. 38, no. 592 (14 February 1918), p.10.

Brief item. *The War Office Topical Budget and Pictorial News* (Official) to be released on 23 February will be devoted exclusively to General Allenby's entry into Jerusalem. In fairness to regular subscribers it has been decided that no orders for single copies will be entertained.

[Pages 28 and 29 of the above number of *The Bioscope* advertises the reel—'The Historic Film of the War'.]

7   ANON. 'Gossip and opinions'. *The Bioscope*, vol. 38, no. 594 (28 February 1918), p.5–7.

On page 7 the columnist writes: 'I hear that the *War Office Topical Budget and Pictorial News* will in future be known as the *Pictorial News (Official)*. The title is an appropriate one, and in its shortened form should add to the popularity and kudos the *Topical Budget* has attained. That it supplies a long-felt want and is appreciated by picture-goers is proved by the fact that the number of copies now issued twice weekly is twice as great as formerly'.

8   ADVERTISEMENT. *The Bioscope*, vol. 40, no. 628 (24 October 1918), p.88–89.

Two-page advertisement for the *Pictorial News*. 'To-day's issue includes Marshall Haig, Gen. Byng and Gen. Horne in Cambrai: historic entry of the British Commander-in-Chief with M. Clemenceau', etc.

1920

9   MALINS, Geoffrey H. *How I filmed the War: a record of the extraordinary experiences of the man who filmed the great Somme battles etc.* Edited by Low Warren. London: Herbert Jenkins, 1920. xii, 307p. illus.

The author, for two years one of the Official War Office Kinematographers gives a detailed and vivid account of how he covered the early years of the First World War. Many illustrations.

1923

10   TALBOT, Frederick A. *Moving pictures: how they are made and worked.* Rev. ed. London: Heinemann, 1923. xiv, 429p.

Chapter 12, 'Moving-picture records of topical events: industrial, interest and scenic films', p.174–188 covers the topics listed. Discusses 'scoops' and the rush to get the news on screen and refers to the importance of library material. The author feels that the topical in the form so widely appreciated ten years earlier has been 'crushed out of existence by the thousand-foot reel'. There are very few subjects capable of sustaining tense interest for sixteen minutes. 'If of shorter length, say 600 feet, then 400 feet of another subject must be added to give the complete reel, and the "split-reel", as such is termed, is not generally appreciated by the public'.

1925

11   ANON. 'Chasing News with a film camera'. *The Picturegoer*, vol. 10, no. 60 (December 1925), p.76.

The news-film cameraman has to be not only a skilled cinematographer and understand the intricacies of all kinds of cinematograph cameras from the ultra-rapid machine to the pneumatic aeroscope but he has to have what is known as news-sense, an appreciation of pictorial values and composition, initiative to get his pictures under great difficulties, imagination and, 'the nerve and pluck to go anywhere and everywhere'. Gaumont Graphic plans stories to be covered for weeks ahead and always has at its disposal a large staff of cameramen who can be sent out immediately when news comes through 'of some great disaster that the public will want to see in pictures'. The Gaumont Graphic reel 'includes about 800 feet of film in its bi-weekly editions and very often these 800 feet constitute the cream of 10,000 feet of negative exposed by the cameramen'. For reference to past events Gaumont Graphic has a library of over 10,000 negatives dating back to 1915.

1927

12   PELHAM, Hugh. 'Those topical boys'. *The Picturegoer*, vol. 14, no. 84 (December 1927), p.22–23.

'Generally speaking, abnormal occurrences such as natural upheavals and phenomena in the form of floods, earthquakes, landslides, eclipses, etc.; current events of outstanding importance, subjects of contemporary interest, of which pictures can be secured, make film news, but an important quality is necessary, and that is the quality of appeal for the majority'. Goes on to look at some of the news-gathering activities of *Pathé Super Gazette's* cameramen, e.g. the cameraman who secured the footage of the Siege of Sidney Street contrived to get through the dense crowd with his camera 'by the desperate but successful expedient of clinging on the back of Mr. Winston Churchill's car'.

1928

13   ANON. 'Short features', *The Bioscope* (18 July 1928), p.54.

Reviews *British Screen News* no. 5, *Eve's Film Reviews* no. 371, *Gaumont Graphic* no. 1807, *Gaumont Mirror* no. 76, *Pathé Pictorial* no. 537 and *Pathé Super Gazette* no. 28–57. *British Screen News* is welcomed as a 'distinct acquisition to the weekly news-reels'. (Note: At this time *The Bioscope* reviewed newsreels and cinemagazines regularly.)

14   ANON. 'Talk of the trade ... The "Tatler's" first appearance'. *The Bioscope* (8 August 1928), p.15.

Last item in column: brief. Welcomes the first edition of *British Screen Tatler* which appeared that week, edited by Charles R. Martin. The reel was produced by British Screen Productions.

15   ANON. 'Short features'. *The Bioscope* (15 August 1928), p.40.

Reviews the 13th issue of *British Screen News*, the 2nd issue of *British Screen Tatler*, no.375 of *Eve's Film Review*, no. 1815 of *Gaumont Graphic*; no. 80 of *Gaumont Mirror*; no. 541 of *Pathé Pictorial* and no. 28–65 of *Pathé Super Gazette*.

1930

16   CHESMORE, Stuart. *Behind the cinema screen*. London: Thomas Nelson, 193–? x, 100p. (Discovery Books series, no.5).

Chapter 5, 'The news in pictures' tells how the newsreels are produced, with particular reference to coverage of annual events like the Boat Race, the Cup Final and Trooping the Colour. There is a two-page section on 'interviewing famous people'.

An early Cup Final (still courtesy of National Film Archive)

17   SIMPSON, Celia. 'The Cinema'. *The Spectator* (22 February 1930), p.268–9.

Briefly contrasts the contents of British and American newsreels with specific examples, including a *British Movietone News* story showing Stanley Baldwin in his library pleading a political cause. The author would prefer to see current interesting events like 'an eruption of Krakatoa' or 'Admiral Byrd in New America', rather than 'personalities in the public eye'. In England one sees too many foundation stones being laid, mayoral functions, drilling troops, inaugural ceremonies and winning football teams. Suggests that the section of current news be supplemented by another section called 'How others live'. Doubts whether sound newsreels are always more successful than their silent precedessors: there is now a tendency to choose subjects which are only remarkable for the sounds which accompany them.

1931

18   LEJEUNE, Caroline Alice. *Cinema*. London: Alexander Maclehose, 1931. x, 255p.

'The News-Theatre', p.208–215 welcomes the establishment of newsreel and magazine theatres, 'one of the most hopeful signs for the future of the cinema'. 'It shows that the industry has grasped, at last, the overwhelming force of the movie as a modern narrator and propagandist . . . But the very fact that such theatres are coming into existence suggests that the news-reels and short film programmes will have to be chosen with much greater care and intelligence, and arranged with much finer sensibility, than they have been in the past'.

1932

19   BUCHANAN, Andrew. *Films: the way of the cinema*. London: Pitman, 1932. xvi, 235p. (Art and Life series).

Chapter 7, 'The interest film: how it is made—ideas men—the news-reel—screen journalism—the cartoon—the advertisement film and the public,' p.185–209, covers the topics listed. The writer feels that it is debateable whether the newsreel editors 'have as yet truly discovered what does and does not constitute news in the screen sense of the word'. 'The newsreel in its present form satisfies the public, and consequently there is no sound reason for altering its policy unless an urge is felt to mould it more carefully to the requirements of the screen, and take advantage of the opportunities which the medium of the film offers. This would necessitate news-reel editors revising their whole method of approach, firstly by realising that there is no similarity between Fleet Street and Wardour Street'.

20   ANON. 'The romance of the newsreel'. *The Picturegoer*, vol. 1, no. 49 (New series), (30 April 1932), p.12–13.

'The smuggling of celluloid "scoops" with the aid of feminine confederates, picture piracy, with prison as a penalty for the unlucky, and thrilling road and air races with the news spools are all part of the day's work to the modern cameraman-reporter'. For the newsreel company shut out by an 'exclusive rights' deal there are three alternatives. 'One, to pirate the picture with silent cameras and put sound on to it from the library. Two, to fake a picture and issue it before the "exclusive rights" holder gets his authentic films out, and three, to ignore the event entirely and concentrate on some other news story'. Most newsreels now own a sound track library but when they first began good sound tracks were few and far between, e.g. one firm who owned a specially good crowd track put it on every crowd scene they issued. It was easily recognisable to anyone in the trade because at a certain point a dog barked.

21   GAMMIE, John. 'What's wrong with this week's newsreels?' *Film Weekly*, vol. 8, no. 211 (28 October 1932), p.7.

The journal's review editor gives as his three essentials for a good newsreel, topicality, variety and originality of viewpoint. Few of the items released at the beginning of that week fulfilled more than one of these conditions. Goes on to review the main stories. Advises the newsreels to avoid showing with monotonous regularity such items as 'ships being launched; troops being reviewed; charters being presented; wreaths being laid, anniversaries being celebrated; and Swiss cavalry performing manoeuvres'. In an accompanying column the magazine asks its readers: 'What did *you* think of the various items in the newsreels described and criticised by our review editor?'

22   GAMMIE, John. 'New ideas for the newsreels: "Film Weekly" readers join in our compaign'. *Film Weekly*, vol. 8, no. 212 (4 November 1932), p.11.

Reports that the general opinion of *Film Weekly* readers in their response to the writer's 'Better Newsreels Campaign' which he started the previous week is that 'newsreels certainly *have* been dull lately, but with a few improvements and additions . . . could easily be one of the brightest and best features of the average programme'. Goes on to give a selection of the opinions received. In a separate box, the author reviews 'this week's best' stories. Praises Paramount's coverage of the Hunger Marchers in London—the disturbances at Hyde Park during which the mounted police charged rioters with drawn batons: 'The commentary, moreover, was sensible and restrained, emphasising the coolness of the police in tackling the situation'.

23   GAMMIE, John. 'Better newsreels campaign: should newsreels be censored? A reply to the Editor of *British Movietone News*'. *Film Weekly*, vol. 8, no. 213 (11 November 1932), p.11.

Reports that Gerald Sanger, Editor of *British Movietone News*, who replied to some of the opinions expressed in the 'campaign for better and brighter newsreels, considers that newsreel editors should censor their own work by eliminating anything which in their opinion is not in the public interest'. Sanger cites the recent hunger marcher disturbances as a case in point: 'The exhibition of the pictures showing the clashes which took place in Hyde Park will undoubtedly exacerbate the situation, and it is for this reason that the editors of British Newsreels either forebore to cover the subject or to release such pictures as they obtained'. Gammie then goes on to take issue with 'the patriotic idea behind this form of self-censorship' and states that 'it is surely in the public interest that the full truth about the disturbances should be known'. Concludes: 'Newsreel censorship, in my opinion, should be applied mainly to gruesome and revolting subjects'.

24   CUMMINS, G. Thomas. 'What a newsreel editor thinks'. *Film Weekly*, vol. 8, no. 214 (18 November 1932), p.10.

In a letter Cummins welcomes the campaign of *Film Weekly* which he is reading 'with great care'. He expects to gather a great deal of valuable ideas from the letters. He points out some of the differences between newsreels and newspapers particularly with regard to space availability.

25   GAMMIE, John. 'Better newsreels campaign: Women *are* interested in newsreels'. *Film Weekly*, vol. 8, no. 214 (18 November 1932), p.10.

The writer reports that more than half those who wrote in response to his campaign were women. Summarises that the three things in newsreels that women object to most are: 'Impersonal subjects, such as aeroplane experiments and demonstrations of uninteresting machines of various kinds; pictures of pugilists in training, prize fights, wrestling matches, and sport in general; scenes of tragedies and fatal accidents'. Concludes: 'It all comes back to the old newspaper theory (which has never been improved upon) that women are interested in people rather than *things*'.

26 ANON. 'Politics on the screen'. *Kinematograph Weekly*, (13 April 1933), p.43.

Brief item quotes Herbert Morrison, ex-Minister of Transport: 'At the L.C.C. I have called attention to items included in a news film two weeks running in London kinemas which appeared to me to encourage Fascist mob militarism. The people who are responsible for these news films have no right to glorify the Hitler Hate Brigade or to make opportunities for the British Fascist organisation to put a spokesman on the screen praising the Fascism of Italy and Germany and expressing the hope that England will be next. This kind of irresponsibility will bring the kinema into disrepute; it has already enough to answer for . . .'

27 ANON. 'How your news is rushed to you' *Picturegoer*, vol. 2, no. 101 (New series) (29 April 1933), p.11.

Picture piracy has been developed into a fine art, as a result of the "exclusive rights" system which has only come into operation since the intensification of the news reel war brought about by the coming of sound. 'To-day's Cup Final' is a case in point. For days, Movietone executives have been at work at Wembley, not only choosing the best points of vantage for their own cameras, but to make the ground as "camera-proof" as possible for their rivals. Battalions of police and the staff are usually detailed to watch for suspicious-looking parcels that might conceal unauthorised cameras. As the pirates have to work under difficulties the rights holder almost invariably shoots the best and most complete record. Goes on to describe how film is speedily transported by land, sea and air.

28 ANON. 'Leeds fights against cut prices: special conference of exhibitors to be arranged: co-operation with renters suggested'. *Kinematograph Weekly*, (4 May 1933), p.13.

Reports the proceedings of the previous Friday's meeting of the (CEA?) Leeds and District Branch. An item under the heading 'News-reel politics' reads: 'Reporting on the last meeting of the General Council, Mr (C. P.) Metcalfe said a number of branches had taken exception to some of the scenes and some of the dialogue in *Paramount News*—notably in connection with a speech of Sir Oswald Mosley's on Fascism, which was regarded as being altogether wrong. Audiences in many kinemas strongly resented this sort of thing. The General Council had made strong representations to Paramount on the subject, and exhibitors throughout the country were urged to bring to the notice of their branches anything of this nature in a news-reel which they regarded as objectionable'.

29 ANON. 'More newsreel'. *Sight & Sound*, vol. 2, no. 7 (Autumn 1933), p.81.

Two brief items. 1. Reports that the newsreel is making rapid strides in popularity. There are welcome signs that the trade is alive to the demand for more and better reels, e.g., Paramount's international newsreel service is to be improved by special editing of foreign items; Western Electric has designed a new and easily-portable sound camera for newsreel work and Fox Photos Ltd. (well-known press photographers) have inaugurated at a very reasonable price a monthly newsreel service for material taken by 16mm. cameras. (If the latter develops on a large scale it should mean greater facilities for processing 16mm. stock and the consequent removal of one of the chief objections to the use of sub-standard cameras by professionals). 2. The opening of the Victoria Station News Theatre by Norman Hulbert, Managing Director of British News Theatres Ltd. is noted. Various items of information about the construction of the theatre are given. Programmes last 50 minutes. Prices are 6d. between mid-day and 4 p.m. and 1s. from 4 to 11 p.m. On Sundays the theatre is open from 6 p.m. to 11 p.m.

30   FRASER, Donald. 'Newsreel: reality or entertainment?' *Sight & Sound*, vol. 2, no. 7 (Autumn 1933), p.89–90.

Suggests that there is a growing interest by the general public in actuality film—'The erection of another newsreel theatre in Victoria Station brings the number of theatres interested solely in realities to eight in England'. But accuses the newsreels of having a profound interest in superficialities and of showing an excessive number of military scenes, especially parades. Believes that the newsreels strive to be impartial though 'a Fascist influence is discernable at times'. Technically there is too much reliance on the 'safety' shot and editing is bad. Cause is rooted in the attitude of the commercial movie industry to actualities and documentary. Newsreels and shorts are regarded as fill-ups and are not profitable enough. Suggests more control by editor as a way of improving technical standards—the cameraman should be sent out with a scenario and each story should be constructed as a small film in itself. 'A Northcliffe of newsreels, who will lift the newsreel out of its present derelict rut is yet to be born'. A host of subjects await serious coverage and analysis.

31   CARSTAIRS, John Paddy. 'Those news reel scenes'. *Picturegoer*, vol. 3, no. 118 (New series) (26 August 1933), p.8.

Asks—'Are filmgoers tired of the talkie topical treadmill: college steeplechases, Royalty shaking hands with football teams, firemen's championships, carnivals and races?' The author feels that some of the items of interest in the newsreels are becoming 'alarmingly monotonous': the editors of the reels should search more extensively for novel material for their product. Goes on to list stock newsreel scenes.

32   MacDONALD, Alister G. 'News cinema in Victoria Station'. *The Architect's Journal*, vol. 78, (14 September 1933), p.313, 321–5.

Architectural plans, supplemented by photographs of the interior, of the Newsreel Theatre at Victoria Station, designed by MacDonald and opened to the public on the previous Tuesday.

33   ANON. 'News Kinema, Victoria Station, London, S.W.—Architect: Alister G. MacDonald, A.R.I.B.A'. *The Architect & Building News*, vol. 135 (22 September 1933), p.332–5.

Review of the theatre with photographs of the interior and exterior and architectural drawings.

34   *Kinematograph Weekly*. Leading article. 'Politics on the screen'. (26 October 1933), p.4.

'There is not an exhibitor in the country who will defend the policy of letting political views intrude upon the screen. The C.E.A. has repeatedly protested against it. Newsreel editors have acknowledged the justice of these protests. And yet from time to time we get enthusiastic politicians trying to get their lessons preached to audiences who may or may not agree with them, but do very definitely realise that while there is a time and a place for all things, political propaganda in a kinema entertainment is an offence . . .'

35   ANON. 'Propaganda in news reels: Lloyd George makes way for Sir John Simon'. *Kinematograph Weekly*, (26 October 1933), p.3.

Brief item. Reports that a film interview with David Lloyd George was deleted from a newsreel as screened at Gaumont-British theatres the previous week. The ex-Prime Minister in an interview expressed the opinion that the Powers had broken their pledge to Germany in the matter of disarmament as they had not disarmed as agreed. Lloyd George's former Cabinet colleague, Sir John Simon occupied a prominent place in the *Gaumont Graphic* of the same date, claiming that Britain and other signatories had pledged themselves to armament reduction, that Britain had reduced her forces to the edge of a risk, and discussed results of the failure of the Disarmament Conference.

36   ANON. 'Trade union protest: propaganda in news-reels'. *Kinematograph Weekly*, (26 October 1933), p.3.

Brief item. Ernest Bevin protests at an election meeting against the use of the newsreels for political propaganda. Referring to the reel showing Lloyd George Bevin said: 'Even when you come to such places as this for your amusement you are faced with propaganda which is aimed against your own class, and I appeal to you to show resentment against such tactics. When you see your Lord Lloyds and similar people shown to you in the news-reels, hiss them off'.

37   HULBERT, Norman J. 'News films and their public'. *Sight & Sound*, vol. 2, no. 8 (Winter 1933–34), p.132–33.

An article by the Managing Director of British News Theatre Ltd. Takes editors to task for not including enough 'news' in the newsreels yet advises them that 'politics should be sparingly included'. Exhorts editors to 'content themselves with giving us the ungarnished screen stories of the world happening in sound and picture'. Comments briefly on competition between the newsreel companies, exhibition, and the advent of the news theatre.

1934

38   ANON. 'What is a news-reel? Hold-up at Movietone [News] Theatre'. *Kinematograph Weekly*, (8 March 1934), p.3.

Brief item. Vernon Bartlett's 'talk item', "Europe in Ferment" was withheld from the public on 5 March until after the L.C.C. Entertainments Committee and Edward Shortt, the chairman of the British Board of Film Censors had, at their request, seen it in the afternoon. Mr Shortt was asked to decide whether the picture came under the category of topical newsreels 'which are exempt from censorship'. Mr Shortt declined to give a ruling on this point. But he declared that if the item was subject to his censorship he would have no hesitation in passing it. At his suggestion the title was altered to "Europe To-day". 'There is no present intention of showing the picture elsewhere'. Foreign Office officials, ambassadors, etc. attended the Monday evening screening at which Mr Bartlett spoke.

39   CUMMINS, G. Thomas. 'Can newsreels be censored?' *Kinematograph Weekly*, (8 March 1934), p.4.

The Editor of *British Paramount News* outlines his objections to any official form of censorship for the newsreels. From his point of view the most important objection to control is 'its practicability'. 'After authenticity the biggest factor in newsreel operation is speed' and he does not see 'how any form of increased control could do otherwise than hopelessly slow down the publication of screen news'. Gives an example of how Paramount lost a recent scoop of the Paris disturbances because of diplomatic representations which delayed the release of the pictures for two days.

40   ANON. 'Important newsreel case: recording of incidental music challenged'. *Kinematograph Weekly*, (8 March 1934), p.3.

The right of reproduction of music incidental to a topical incident shot by a newsreel has been challenged by music publishers in the High Court. The musical work involved is 'Colonel Bogey'. F. K. Archer, K.C., for the defendants stated that these news films were really the newspaper of the Trade and the defendants were making a perfectly fair use of the work in question. What they were doing, in effect, was to put it in their newspaper and they desired an authoritative ruling as to whether such news films came within the exceptions provided for in the Copyright Act.

41   ANON. 'Newsreels co-operate: Movietone and G-B agreement: Grand National scoop'. *Kinematograph Weekly*, (5 July 1934), p.5, 23.

At a dinner it was announced that Movietone and Gaumont-British have together secured the exclusive rights to film the 1935 Grand National. The item continues on page 23 under the heading 'News-reel censorship: Movietone Chief on liberty: "must be free"', and reports a reference by Gerald F. Sanger to 'the menace of censorship'. 'It is up to us', he went on, 'to correct any disposition to impose any form of censorship on news-reels. News-reels should be as free as the Press and the discretion of editors of newsreels, who are experienced people, should be trusted, neither to outrage the feelings of the public or to attach to the film any commentary that was likely to inflame the public. There have been attempts recently to put a certain amount of pressure upon news-reels and to restrict our activities and functions, that we must resist'.

42   ANON. 'What are topical films? Questions raised by Censors' delayed report'. *Kinematograph Weekly*, (16 August 1934), p.11.

The question whether or not certain 'topical' films should be subject to censorship is dealt with in the Report of the British Board of Film Censors published the previous week. The Board has decided that topical films taken over a period of time and strung together with a running commentary in order to provide a 'story' will be subject to censorship, such films coming within the conditions issued by local authorities.

43   RITCHIE, David. 'That news-reel villainy', *Sight & Sound*, vol. 3, no. 11 (Autumn 1934), p.113–4.

Outlines the result of a quick survey of the subject matter of the newsreels screened in the month of February 1933. Of 296 stories viewed, 30% dealt with sport, 13% with military matters, 3% with activities of Royalty, 3% with other ceremonials, 30% with travel and political, social, commercial or industrial interest and 21% with miscellaneous items. Geographical distribution of items was as follows: G.B. and Northern Ireland 37%; British Empire and Irish Free State $7^1/_2$%; U.S.A. 20%; Europe $28^1/_2$%; Japan $3^1/_2$% and Rest of the World $3^1/_2$%. Only 35% of the total number of items had any 'real topical pictorial news-value'. Comments on the preponderance of men in news-theatre audiences and briefly on problems of editors and on the effects of censorship on the future use of the newsreel as historical records.

44   MacDONALD, Alister G. 'News theatre at Waterloo Station'. *The Architects' Journal*, vol. 80, (6 September 1934), p.322–27.

Architectural plans, supplemented by photographs of the interior and exterior of the News Theatre at Waterloo Station, designed by MacDonald and opened to the public the previous week.

45   ANON. 'The Waterloo Station News Theatre—Architect: Alister G. MacDonald, F.R.I.B.A.' *The Architect & Building News*, vol. 139 (7 September 1934), p.273–5.

Brief review of the theatre with photographs of the interior and exterior and architectural plans.

46   ANON. 'News Theatre Waterloo Station, S.E.: Mr. Alister G. MacDonald, A.R.I.B.A., Architect'. *The Builder*, vol. 147 (14 September 1934), p.433–5.

Architectural plans with photographs of the interior and exterior.

47   ANON. 'Editing and presenting film "copy": the great improvements in editorial technique and other factors in the production of brighter news films', by a Newsreel Editor. *Kinematograph Weekly* (25 October 1934), News Reel and Shorts Supplement, p.20.

The newly-opened Waterloo Station News Theatre in 1934. See abstract no. 45 (Photo courtesy of the British Architectural Library)

Much of the development of the newsreel has resulted from improved sound recording and increased facility in the use of sound. Discusses titling and use of music. With regard to publishing 'there are conflicting views as to the advisability of assembling all the stories for the two weekly issues on Mondays and Wednesdays, or of spreading the selection over the week', as is the writer's practice. Discusses the pros and cons. Finally discusses the use of colour.

48   ANON. 'Wanted—a name! suggested titles for kinemas showing interest films'. *Kinematograph Weekly*, (25 October 1934), News Reel and Shorts Supplement, p.20.

In news theatres now only about one third of the programme is devoted to actual news, the rest being made up of interest and cartoon films and often a two-reel comedy. 'To a large number of people the news is the chief attraction, but there are those who endure the news for the sake of the rest of the programme; this type may possibly be found more among the less intelligent section of the public, but after all their money is worth as much at the pay-box. The term "interest theatre" appeals as a good alternative (to "news theatre" as a generic title). Then there is the desirability of characteristic names for individual interest theatres. Suggested names include, "The Hour Glass", "The Almanach", "World Wide", "The Times", "Passing Shows"'.

49   CUMMINS, G. Thomas. 'Telling the world with pictures: views on the question of censorship and exclusive rights'. *Kinematograph Weekly*, (25 October 1934), News Reel and Shorts Supplement, p.8.

The author, Editor of *British Paramount News*, feels that the reponsibilities of running a newsreel have never been heavier than they are now. The editor has to endeavour to appreciate the tastes of the largest majority and to satisfy them all. 'Propaganda is forbidden.

Partiality is prescribed and parochialism is taboo. The daily life of the whole civilized world is to be told in pictures, nothing must be omitted. But nothing must be included which the average man will not like. We do not hope to satisfy these conditions—they represent an ideal—but we have to get as near as possible'. The idea that newsreels should be made subject to a form of censorship is neither desirable nor would it be practicable without placing serious difficulties in the way of the newsreels, slowing down their speed of operation until the news value of almost every story would be killed. With regard to 'exclusive rights', he has been standing firm upon the principle that newsreels should be accorded precisely the same treatment as newspapers in regard to the coverage of public news events. In practically every other country the newsreels have established their claim to equal treatment.

50   DITCHAM, S. F. 'Universal's newsreel policy'. *Kinematograph Weekly* (25 October 1934), News Reel and Shorts Supplement, p.12.

The Managing Director of *Universal Talking News* breezily outlines future plans for this reel. Conjointly with *Pathé Gazette* and *British Paramount News*, Universal for the first time has signed exclusive rights to film the Cup Final in 1935; every means is being employed to keep the service 'bang up to date'; Universal's policy of having the news fully commentated on a background of sound' will continue, etc.

51   HALES DUTTON, H. 'Documentary, propaganda and travel films: they are all "news"-reels!' *Kinematograph Weekly* (25 October 1934), News Reel and Shorts Supplement, p.27.

'At first glance the parallel between the so-called interest film and the newsreel would appear somewhat obscure. A little reflection, however, must convince us that the basis of all documentary, instructional or propaganda films is fundamentally the same as that of the newsreel—Truth. The essence of every newsreel is accuracy and freedom from any professional touch whatever, apart from the skill and daring of the cameramen'. Agrees with Paul Rotha that 'newsreels are simply an up-to-the-minute expression of the documentary film'. 'The mushroom growth of news theatres and their extraordinary success are the best proof that films dealing with real life, whether in a British steel foundry, or the death of a king are of the deepest interest to the general public'. Bigger and better documentary films should also be produced 'so that the almost insatiable demand of the public may be satisfied'. The newsreel and the documentary are 'the screen corollary of the newspaper with the 2,000,000 circulation'.

52 · HULBERT, Norman. 'What I demand of the newsreel editor'. *Kinematograph Weekly*, (25 October 1934), News Reel and Shorts Supplement, p.5.

The author, Managing Director of British News Theatres, writes, 'The news film is the greatest propaganda medium in the world, not even excluding broadcasting, for in the latter case it is easy to "switch off", but when a news film is sandwiched between two feature films in a programme, I defy anyone to turn a deaf ear or a blind eye to its exhibition, and in this the newsreel editor has us at his mercy'. Editors, however, have a great deal to learn. Politics should be 'very sparsely' included, unless the newsreel is going to ally itself to any particular Party which is to be abhorred. It is almost impossible to treat political talks impartially. Efforts have been made to secure a talk by each party leader for inclusion in one news film, but results have never been completely satisfactory. Editors should content themselves with giving the unvarnished screen stories of the world happenings in sound and picture. The bargaining by newsreel companies for the exclusive rights to film certain events is an appalling waste of money. Newsreels are included in ordinary cinema programmes occupying about 5% of the programme or are screened in small theatres devoted exclusively to the presentation of newsreel and shorts, 'an entirely new departure'. Goes on to discuss siting, programming and audiences for these news theatres.

53   JEFFREY, R. E. 'My job as a commentator: an amazing record of five thousand news stories'. *Kinematograph Weekly*, (25 October 1934), News Reel and Shorts Supplement, p.12.

A day in the life of the well-known commentator whose three golden rules of commentating are, 1) Be yourself; 2) Be natural; 3) Be yourself, and be natural. The best commentators are born, not made.

54   MacDONALD, Alister. 'Planning the modern news theatre'. *Kinematograph Weekly*, (25 October 1934), News Reel and Shorts Supplement, p.13–15.

In an interview, MacDonald, the Premier's son, discusses the architecture of the news theatre. A news theatre should seat from 250 to 350 patrons. It should be intimate; and easy to walk in or out of, as people continuously pass in and out—for example, in his Victoria Station theatre 100 people pass in and out every hour throughout the day. No seat must be far from a gangway. A 'cosy light' is another requirement in an auditorium where there is a good deal of moving about. The regulation which limits a slope to a pitch of 1 in 10 should be liberally interpreted in many circumstances. A mirror projection system gives protection against eyestrain and distorted images. Reference is made to news theatres in Paris and Amsterdam. He foresees news theatres extending their service: 'every community centre, every recreational club of any size will be having its news theatre in some form or another. Television will be tried in news theatres first, when this branch of science is more advanced'. Includes two architectural drawings of the Waterloo Station News Theatre.

55   SANGER, Gerald F. 'The programme of a news theatre: how it should be treated and presented'. *Kinematograph Weekly*, (25 October 1934), News Reel and Shorts Supplement, p.15.

The article is based on an interview with Gerald Sanger of *British Movietone News*. 'The appellation—news theatre—is so loosely applied nowadays that it has almost become a misnomer. Many of the so-called news theatres are in reality shorts theatres, where the preponderance of the programme consists of interest films . . . A disadvantage of the type of programme offered by the "shorts" theatre is the problem arising from duplication of various newsreel versions of the same subject. The more important the news covered, the more certain does duplication become'. Editing by the exhibitors becomes necessary. This 'temporary unofficial editing' is winked at by the newsreel companies. The news theatre programme is quite different, 'with its systematised forty-minute picture news service strengthened with the introduction of special news "featurettes" and interspersed with screen talks by various well-known people. The classic example of such a perfected news theatre service is to be found in the programme put on at the Shaftesbury Pavilion and, *at the moment*, to be seen nowhere else. Its editing, sub-titles and subject matter are all of them exclusive'. Since 1930 this theatre, managed by Leslie Landau, has acted as a nursery for news theatre managers.

56   SIMMONDS, Roy. 'Newsreels of the future'. *Kinematograph Weekly*, (25 October 1934), News Reel and Shorts Supplement, p.4.

The main appeal of newsreels is *news*. There is a real analogy between a newsreel and a newspaper. News is most interesting, attractive and thrilling when it is actually happening. The newsreel of the future will show 'red-hot' news. In the not too distant future live newsreels will co-operate with live theatre managements and utilise television as an adjunct to the newsreel as it is now known. 'Television, of course, will not supplant the celluloid reel for many obvious reasons'.

57   BISHOP, H. W. 'Newsreel in the making', *Sight & Sound*, vol. 3, no. 12 (Winter 1934–35), p.150–52.

An article by the Production Manager of Gaumont-British News. Discussing the criteria for selecting stories for the newsreels—'pictorial news with action', e.g. launching of ships, air displays; 'forbidden subjects' e.g. 'controversial news' and 'crime'—production difficulties, e.g. need to obtain permission for filming, insurance, camera position, editing.

1935

58   BUCHANAN, Andrew. 'Toward the newsreel of the future. 1: News reels or real news,' *Film Art*, vol. 3, no. 7 (1935), p. 22–24.

Points out current success of the newsreel in terms of circulation and revenue then asks, 'What is the matter with the commercial newsreel?'. The various newsreels are broadly speaking identical, with a conventional form of presentation that indicates a lack of originality. Realises difficulties under which newsreel staffs work and feels that the newsreel as it is constituted under existing conditions cannot be changed. Urges the creation of more analytical comment as exemplified by *The March of Time* and the previous year's *Gaumont News* presentation on the Armistice. Feels that a twice weekly release invites too much padding with non-topical material and deplores the 'pandering to national traditions', e.g. military forces forever being praised.

59   MOORE, John C. 'Toward the newsreel of the future. 2: The cameraman's approach,' *Film Art*, vol. 3, no. 7 (1935), p.24–26.

Accuses the newsreel 'in its present form' of lacking all advanced technique of filmcraft and reducing the role of the newsreel camerman to that of a photographer. Stresses the need for good use of camera angle and more judicious editing.

60   NICHOLSON, Irene. 'Toward the newsreel of the future. 3: News reel comment,' *Film Art*, vol. 3, no. 7 (1935), p.26–27.

States that it is utterly impossible in news film to avoid some form of editorial comment for not only the choice of news but the angles, lighting and juxtaposition of shots are in their very nature subjective. Briefly discusses the reception of *The March of Time* in Britain and compares it to a weekly news magazine. The American cinemagazine should give the lead to a more reasonable film journalism.

61   ANON. 'Entertainment and realism: Paramount's progressive newsreel policy'. *Kinematograph Weekly*, (28 March 1935). Shorts & News Reel Supplement, p.27.

A review of the work and organisation of *British Paramount News* which 'has recently celebrated its fourth anniversary'. The newsreel has 'intensified its policy of covering the maximum number of major news stories and excluding from the reel everything purely decorative in effect or of a fill-up character'. Concludes with a list of 'outstanding' Paramount stories.

62   ANON. 'The Grand National: how Gaumont-British will film it: 250 newsreelmen on parade'. *Kinematograph Weekly*, (28 March 1935). Shorts & News Reels Supplement, p.22.

Describes the plans for covering the event and getting the reel to the cinemas. The newsreel company 'will concentrate over 250 cameramen and details on and around the 16 jumps' and expects to expose at least 10,000 feet of negative stock 'making cutting and editing a colossal task'. Jeffrey Bernerd and Castleton-Knight will be in charge of the operation.

63   ANON. 'Is news enough? Stereotyped newsreel presentation. "*March of Time*" experiment'. *Kinematograph Weekly*, (28 March 1935). Shorts & News Reels Supplement, p.14.

The real showman should not underestimate the value of the newsreel as a 'patronage builder'. 'A reputation for the presentation of news when it is news has proved a definite financial asset to many a kinema'. The organisation and production of the modern reel has made great advances, however, 'progress on these lines has not been accompanied with similar development in make-up of the general editorial presentation of the various news items'. The presentation of the sound newsreel has become essentially stereotyped. Various experiments represent 'gropings toward a new formula'. But there has been a 'return to the straightforward screening of world happenings which follow the usual cycle of royal progresses, sporting events, and the aftermath of disaster, linked together by a few bars of musical introduction or the wisecracks of a commentator'. 'The duty of the newsreel editor is to provide the patron with news uncoloured and free from personal or political bias . . .' 'Presentation of news should be invested with more imagination'. Goes on to favourably discuss the *March of Time* and concludes that the significance of this new development should not be ignored 'for this method of presenting contemporary history at least does provide the basis of a fresh formula for news treatment on the screen'.

64   ANON. '*Pathé Gazette* forges ahead: new equipment still further improves service'. *Kinematograph Weekly*, (28 March 1935). Shorts & News Reels Supplement, p. 20.

Brief review of the progress of the Pathé organisation. 'The commentary in every issue (of its reel) is 100 per cent real entertaining talk and not just a straight-laced string of sentences announced indifferently'. An average of 18,000 miles per week is covered by Pathé cameramen. With regard to the 'periodicals' *Pathétone Weekly* and *Pathé Pictorial*, 'the novel, the amusing and the strange are persistently sought after, and the subjects are carefully chosen to appeal to all tastes'.

65   ANON. 'The romance of Movietone: scoops of the pioneer sound newsreel'. *Kinematograph Weekly* (28 March 1935). Shorts & News Reels Supplement, p.26.

A review of the work and organisation of Movietone. Figures five an idea of the scale, e.g. in the first seven years of its existence *British Movietone News* has exhibited almost 800,000 feet of film, and upwards of 7 million feet, collected from all over the world, have been exposed. The Movietone organisation has five publication centres around the world and issues special newsreels for 36 countries and 100 million people. Some British Movietone personnel are named.

66   ANON. 'The technique of the commentator: a journalistic analogy by "Kinevox".' *Kinematograph Weekly* (28 March 1935). Shorts & News Reels Supplement, p.15.

Discusses the art of the commentator. He is a reporter. 'He tells his audience by means of a film sound track, the story of the picture that is being shown' . . . 'Commentary in newsreels, to be successful, must . . . be essentially informative, clear in wording, bright yet interesting, decisive in style and typically English. The American style of high speed, rapid fire bombarding of the ears with cascades of words, words, and more words is not wanted on the screens which show British newsreels' . . . 'Presentation of commentary in newsreels is as of great importance as the script . . .'

67   DAVIES, C. O. 'If Hore-Belisha were C.E.A. President! A discourse on shorts and speeds by an exhibitor who has cut newsreels from his programmes at one theatre'. *Kinematograph Weekly* (28 March 1935). Shorts & News Reels Supplement, p.10.

In discussing the financial aspects of cinema programming the author complains that there is so little opportunity of bringing in any extra money at the box office with a newsreel that many exhibitors have ceased to include it in their programmes. 'Firstly, the cost is fairly prohibitive, as the renter has a very strong objection to making any allowance for the news, as a general rule, when renting a programme on percentage. Secondly, so much stock magazine matter is included that, compared with items of actual news value, it is not usually worth the price asked for it, especially as the exhibitor has to book it for a period, being in the dark as to whether he will receive any worth-while news items during this period'. Asks why the Cinema Exhibitors' Association does not produce its own newsreel.

68   SANGER, Gerald F. 'Developments in news presentation: departmentalisation and dramatisation'. *Kinematograph Weekly* (28 March 1935). Shorts & News Reels Supplement, p.17.

The Editor of *British Movietone News* having just returned from a trip to the United States analyses the progress made in the production of American newsreels. He found three main advances: 'star' commentators, departmentalisation and dramatisation.

69   WATTS, Freddy. 'Variety the spice of to-day's newsreel: the search for new presentation methods'. *Kinematograph Weekly*, (28 March 1935). Shorts & News Reels Supplement, p.21.

Brief review by the Pathétone Studios Studio Manager, stressing the growth in length of the newsreel over the years from 350 feet to a minimum of 850 feet. Concludes: 'The newsreel cannot go back; it must adapt and improve itself to suit the ever-changing conditions of to-day and to-morrow'.

70   ANON. 'The news-reel war: production costs mounting by "Ex-Ray".' *The Journal of the Association of Cine-Technicians*, vol. 1, no. 1 (May 1935), p.2.

Conditions of employment, salaries, allowances and expenses have been drastically cut to allow for excessive spending on exclusive film rights—an expenditure of £2,000 on rights not unusual. Attempts to stifle rivals' competition by excluding rival cameramen from national events impossible with new modern hand cameras—'pirates' from the companies can always get their shots in spite of up to 250 heavies hired for protection at an event like the Grand National.

71   ANON. 'Newsreel horrors'. *Film Weekly*, vol. 13, no. 349 (21 June 1935), p.6.

Deprecates the filming by a Universal cameraman of the execution by firing squad of a Cuban rebel. The author writes: 'I cannot see any possible justification for taking pictures of the death of an unimportant Cuban rebel. It isn't "news", being of purely local significance. To the outside world it is just a piece of meaningless horror—and the exhibition of such things in cinemas dedicated to entertainment is not to be encouraged'.

72   ROBERTS, Glyn. 'News-reels'. *The New Statesman and Nation* (7 September 1935), p.304–5.

Documents the arrival of the news-cinemas in Britain beginning with the Avenue Pavilion in London's Shaftesbury Avenue which announced itself as the first house of its kind in Europe. In the West End there are now at least seven and there are ones at Victoria and Waterloo Stations and at Praed Street, near Paddington. Their success is unquestioned. Then goes on to discuss the importance of the newsreels as a medium of propaganda. It is impossible that news on the screen can be given absolutely impersonally and without bias. This being so, it would be far better if the bias were open and admitted. Accuses *British Movietone News* in particular (though the same comments 'often' apply to *Gaumont-British News*) of providing a 'highly tendentious view of the news while suggesting to the average cinema-goer that he is receiving an objective, unbiased visual account of all the news that is fit to print'. 'Lately, the great weight of half-articulate resentment at the failure of the self-styled news-reel companies to fulfil their supposed function has been breaking out in a smattering of pungent and exasperated letters to the general press and to the film-fan weeklies'.

73   PULLAN, W. A. 'Unseen stars of the news reel'. *Picturegoer*, vol. 5, no. 230 (New series) (19 October 1935), p.24.

'The news reel is assuming a new importance compatible with its reputation of being an essential and extremely popular section of the programme. Whereas formerly a news subject was treated by editors as a pictorial story, nowadays commentary by well-known authorities lifts it on a higher plane. Modern commentary serves a twofold purpose. It fills up the gaps, so that explanatory observations make the story concise and compact and it saves footage which means that nine or ten subjects can be included in a reel of 850 feet where formerly four or five were the maximum. The news reel has been speeded up by this combination of image and commentary, and furthermore the crediting of commentators enables the public to learn from what authority the observations they hear emanate'. Goes on to review briefly the skills of commentators such as Sir Malcolm Campbell, G. Ward Price, Tom Webster and Captain R. C. Lyle. Remarks that newsreels 'are as nearly as possible paralleling newspaper make-up' before concluding with some comments on the art of commentating for the newsreel.

74   ATKINSON, Messrs. Robert. 'Movie: (Section) B: Construction. 2: Complete schemes: Eros News Reel, Piccadilly Circus'. *The Architect's Journal*, vol. 82 (7 November 1935), p.690–1. (Special issue of the Journal devoted to the architecture of the cinema. This item is a sub-section of B2.)

Architectural diagrams, supplemented by photographs of the interior, of the Eros News Theatre at Piccadilly Circus, designed by Messrs. Atkinson.

75   MacDONALD, Alister G. 'Movie = (Section) A: Planning. 2: Newsreel'. *The Architect's Journal*, vol. 82 (7 November 1935), p.661–6. (Special issue of the Journal devoted to the architecture of the cinema.)

Analyses, using diagrams and notes, some of the problems connected with the design of a news theatre. MacDonald writes: 'It is not enough that this new form of public entertainment and education should be housed in converted halls where the acoustic and ventilating conditions are adapted, and where the whole compromise is called "modern", because a new pay-box has been installed and the theatre given a fresh coat of paint. The news reel and "shorts" programme must be developed by people of imagination, because the field of presentation is enormous. Exhibitors and the public will be demanding special buildings for this type of entertainment—one might rightly say educative entertainment. The sites must be carefully chosen in busy spots. Values of property dictate that the theatre will have to be enclosed in larger buildings, that the theatre must be individual, and yet be a small part of another building. The plan must conserve space and yet produce a big effect. Ingenuity out of imagination will be the sire of this architecture'.

76   ANON. 'Hot news from Ethiopia: Stallings in charge of Movietone Expedition'. *Kinematograph Weekly*, (14 November 1935). News Reel and Shorts Supplement, p.11.

The development of the Italo-Abyssinian war is foremost in the minds of the public today. Movietone's huge resources have enabled it to send to East Africa camera units which will remain there during the duration of the war. The operation is under the personal supervision of Laurence Stallings, the New York editor and the camera units contain among their personnel many of the leading newsreel photographers in the world today, e.g. Len Hammond, Al Waldron and George Mejat. 'Ten cameras, sound, silent and hand were specially made, while motor trucks with protection compartment were purchased together with a fleet of side-car-equipped motor-cycles. Miniature laboratories for making tests on the ground were designed and built'. Special arrangements have been made to service exhibitors at the earliest possible moment.

77   ANON. 'Newsreel Technicians' Association'. *Kinematograph Weekly*, (14 November 1935), News Reel and Shorts Supplement, p.5.

Brief item announcing that a newsreel section of the Association of Cine-Technicians is in process of formation and will include cameramen and sound engineers, cutters, editorial assistants and commentators. 'A meeting was recently held of these staffs at which a provisional committee was appointed, composed of a sound engineer and cameraman from each of the five newsreels, together with two free-lance newsreel technicians'. Rules and regulations are being drawn up and a general meeting will be held later. The objects of the section are co-operative and educational.

78   ANON. 'Plea for better news presentation: lessons to be learnt from Fleet Street by "Kinevox".' *Kinematograph Weekly*, (14 November 1935), News Reel and Shorts Supplement, p.5.

The man in the street is no longer content with his newspaper: he wants the news in moving pictures as well. Despite the increased growth of public interest, 'manifest by the continual and expanding plans of newsreel theatre owners—a small but enlightened body—the average exhibitor still regards the newsreel as "a necessary evil".' Exhibitors should demand a 'newsreel that lives, that is bright and interesting'. The individual exhibitor must have the right to demand coverage of local or area events. He should break away from the slavery of the 800 foot reel. Newsreels are still far from perfection. Often there is a lack of continuity. 'A reel is the newspaper of the screen and should be produced as such by people who have an instinctive knowledge and training in news, pictorial values of news. News editing in newsreels to-day is a joke. The core of the edition—news—is woefully badly handled and selected'. Cutting and sound need to be improved. 'Commentary on newsreels is going from bad to worse. One reel alone continues to be distinguished for its witty clarity, informative accuracy and information, for its complete lack of forced facetiousness! Accuracy is the first consideration, and one reel in particular is distinguished for its gaffes of inaccuracy'. The author finally calls for better titling and better prints—'the majority of prints shown in theatres to-day leave much to be desired'.

79   ANON. 'World's best variety talent in Pathé periodicals: "service" the keystone of news organisation'. *Kinematograph Weekly*, (14 November 1935). News Reel and Shorts Supplement, p.25.

Eighteen years earlier *Pathé Pictorial*, the first recognised screen magazine appeared. At a later date *Pathétone Weekly* first made its appearance. Through the medium of these weeklies 'the world's most prominent people and all manner of artistes well known on the stage, screen and radio' are shown. Extensive thought and preparation have gone into the wide organisation necessary to ensure a continuous output of ever-varying and novel subjects. A compact, fully-equipped sound-proof studio in London's West End its in constant use: many famous personalities have been filmed there. 'Mobile sound units, special portable recording gear, sunlight arcs, spotlights and filament lights are ready at a moment's notice to secure some outside scoop'. A department is constantly on the lookout for 'meritorious talent' to appear in the Pathé periodicals. 'New camera angles and novel treatment of the more ordinary ideas are adopted. Originality in all things is always the aim of all concerned in the Pathé production department . . . A recent feature in Pathétone is the series of famous League football teams in training and practice, with personal interviews'. The article goes on to interview W. J. Gell, Managing Director of Pathé Pictures Ltd. about the popular success of the newsreel *Pathé Gazette*. Newsreel theatres are opening in most important cities 'which indicate that there exists a vast public of newsreel-conscious people'. Pathé has little need to concern itself with *Pathé Gazette*'s popularity and rather concentrates on improving service to the exhibitor'.

80   CUMMINS, G. Thomas. 'Filming the African War: British Paramount organises for all eventualities'. *Kinematograph Weekly*, (14 November 1935), News Reel and Shorts Supplement, p.16.

'Foresight', the London Editor of *British Paramount News* writes, 'is one of the principal factors in newsreel organisation, and to-day more than ever the newsreel editor has to work ahead—sometimes many months ahead—in order that his men are on the spot when the story breaks'. Due to Paramount's scouts and contact men having been on the alert when Mussolini's soldiers were first landed in Africa nearly twelve months before Paramount's organisation in Abyssinia was established, 'complete and ready for all eventualities, long before the Italian attack commenced'. As a result, it now has not only the means of securing pictures in any part of the country but also the means of getting them out of the country and back to England with the least possible delay. The author then gives names and credentials of the Paramount cameramen, sound-men and administrative personnel on the spot. Among the cameramen, D. Messir, an Italian *Paramount News* staffer is attached to General de Bono and Giordani, another Italian, is covering operations in Italian Somaliland.

81   HUTCHISON, J. H. 'News and featurettes in public demand: essential programme ingredients and why they should be exploited'. *Kinematograph Weekly*, (14 November 1935), News Reel and Shorts Supplement, p.4, 6.

According to the author, Manager of the Ambassadors in Hendon, newsreel theatres are opening every week, and doing fine business selling nothing but news and shorts. 'Vast masses of potential kinema-goers, previously untapped, are paying to see nothing else'. 'Hot news is the most easily sold commodity the world knows'. It is the exhibitor's business to make room in the programme for news. Shorts and interest films must also be publicised more.

82   SANGER, Gerald F. 'Star values in news: kinema patrons welcome new Movietone make-up'. *Kinematograph Weekly*, (14 November 1935). News Reel and Shorts Supplement, p.11.

The Producer of *British Movietone News*, who in the March 1935 News Reel and Shorts Supplement had discussed the departmentalisation and dramatisation of news, now writes about Movietone's policy in this direction. On April 25th the first edition of the new *British Movietone News* was successfully launched. The author compliments the contributors to the revamped reel including among the commentators, Barry Barnes whose 'dialect commentaries have been a source of considerable enjoyment to kinemagoers'. All commentators now receive credit on the title, an innovation which has 'materially assisted in the progress of the reel'. 'The commentary is no longer a voice—a background to the image—but an observation by an expert whose knowlege of that particular subject is recognised'. *British Movietone News* thus now has 'star value'. 'The commentary on Movietone is purely of an explanatory nature, and it should be hardly necessary to stress the fact that *British Movietone News* never has and never will abuse its influence as a news publishing medium to distort the significance of events or to give them propagandist flavour. It is in a public-spirited manner and with complete disinterestedness that Movietone will follow the events of this busy and confused world'.

83   WINNER, Howard. 'Storm over Ethiopia: the adventures of a newsreel cameraman in Abyssinia'. *Kinematograph Weekly*, (14 November 1935), News Reel and Shorts Supplement, p.6.

Brief item by Universal's Staff Chief in Abyssinia. He writes: 'From shooting the Chinese with a motion picture camera, located around Shanghai, I was ordered to take the fastest boats, 'planes, train and cars I could to record the forces of Mussolini and Selassie doing a different kind of shooting'. The Emperor appointed a bodyguard for him and arranged permits for him to go everywhere. The heat of the sun and the mosquitos made working conditions difficult.

1936

84   BUCHANAN, Andrew. *The art of film production*. London: Pitman, 1936. xii, 99p.

Chapter 7, 'News-reels or real news', p.70–75, begins by asking 'what is the matter with the commercial news-reel?' and replies that the reels are identical 'both in the items they include and in their presentation' so there is a lack of originality; the annual stories such as Ascot, the Cup Final, the Armistice ceremony are such 'that the majority of people would be no wiser if last year's events were shown next year' and, 'abbreviated versions of football matches are illogical, and extremely uninteresting'. Goes on to recognise the difficulties of newsreel production. In his final section on 'the news-reel of the future' the author, Editor of the *Gaumont-British Magazine* writes that if the newsreels are to continue at all 'in more enlightened days they will be last-minute films presented *in addition* to carefully made documentary-news productions'. Finally he criticises the way in which the newsreel makers 'pander to national traditions, as do the majority of newspapers'. 'The army, navy and air force are forever being given pictorial praise, and rarely do editors reveal any signs of enlightenment, or that they can see beyond a waving flag'. Concludes: 'One of these days we shall see a really real news-reel—but then, I suppose, the Censor would not like it'.

85   NEWBERRY, G. H. 'Some aspects of news-reel recording'. *The Journal of the Association of Cine-Technicians* (February 1936), p.85–6, 88.

Looks at various aspects of newsreel recording technique as differing from studio technique. Briefly surveys the equipment and the demands made on the equipment of news-reel recording units. Highlights some of the problems of outside recording—liability to wow in very cold weather conditions, wind, background noises, distortion. Concludes with a positive consideration of the challenge presented by the BBC's decision to transmit news on television.

86   BROOM, Andrew. 'Pioneer news-reel theatre is shopwindow for the realists'. *World Film News*, vol. 1, no. 2 (May 1936), p.7.

A brief article by the Manager of the Tatler Theatre, Charing Cross Road, London on the history of that cinema from its opening on Monday, February 16th, 1931 with a programme consisting of a newsreel, magazine, cartoon and 'two-reel interest'. Gives an indication of audience reaction to British documentories, *The March of Time*, and signs of advertising or propaganda.

87   SANGER, Gerald. 'Co-ordinate brains for news-reel says Sanger: evolution of commentary is a thrilling business'. *World Film News*, vol. 1, no. 2 (May 1936), p.20.

An article by the producer of Fox Movietone News. Discusses various aspects of commentary writing and commentating and pleads for greater co-operation with the film editor.

88   ANON. 'Soccer League boycott may follow Cup Final squabble'. *World Film News*, vol. 1, no. 3 (June 1936), p.22.

The newsreel companies between them had offered around £2,000 for the rights to film the game. Wembley Stadium held out for more, so the companies withdrew their first offer and substituted a smaller one. Wembley Stadium retaliated by deciding to make the film themselves with subsequent releasing at £12-10-0 a booking. Newsreel companies hired planes and autogyros which the Stadium tried to ban but as the companies were 'on good terms with the Air Ministry' no flying ban was issued. The newsreels got their pictures using long-focus lenses.

89   CASTLETON-KNIGHT, L. 'Aeroplanes and tape machines cover the world for news-reel'. *World Film News*, vol. 1, no. 3 (June 1936), p.22.

A WFN interview with the Managing-Director of Gaumont-British, Mr Castleton-Knight highlights some of the reasons for the success of *Gaumont-British News* which at that time circulated in 1,750 cinemas throughout Great Britain and Ireland—network of cameramen at home and abroad, tie-up in U.S.A. with Fox Movietone and Hearst News-reel, distribution by air, permanent staff of 27 cameramen with five mobile recording trucks. G.B.'s weekly budget was then about £3,000 for two editions, exclusive of specials which could cost up to £2,000 on rights alone.

90   ANON. 'Sensational Queen Mary newsreel: poor cutting mars crack photography'. *World Film News*, vol. 1, no. 4 (July 1936), p.42.

Tells how *Paramount News* filmed the special on the arrival of the ship in New York and her subsequent voyage home. A documentary rather than snappy news treatment was employed. The reviewers felt that while the camerawork (including aerial shots) was excellent the newsreel suffered because a cutter trained in documentary method was not employed to edit it.

91   WATTS, Fred. 'Pioneer recalls struggles of early newsreel'. *World Film News*, vol. 1, no. 4 (July 1936), p.42.

The writer, Pathétone Studios Studio Manager, briefly looks at the early newsreel period (from 1910), lists the names of many fellow-pioneers, considers subsequent growth and anticipates the arrival of television news.

92   ANON. 'Propaganda in newsreels and "Glebelands": South Wales Discussions'. *Kinematograph Weekly*, (23 July 1936), p.13.

Two-part item. On the question of propaganda in the newsreels Arthur B. Watts reported on the proceedings of the previous C.E.A. General Council meeting when the General Secretary had reported that one newsreel company had inquired whether it would meet with the approval of the C.E.A. in view of previously expressed opinion concerning political propaganda, if speeches by Cabinet Ministers were included in newsreels. The Council agreed that when such speeches were definitely of news value the Association would not raise objections to their inclusion. R. Dooner reported that the newsreel companies had been consulted and the Council hoped in the future to prevent, or at least reduce, any objectionable political propaganda from the screen. (Regarding the second part of the item "Glebelands" was the convalescent and rest home recently presented to the Cinematograph Trade Benevolent Fund by Sir William Jury and opened on 8 July 1936.)

93   ANON. 'George Noble (no. 2 of Cameramen series)'. *World Film News*, vol. 1, no. 5 (August 1936), p.41.

A profile of the above named cameraman who in the early years of his career worked on the newsreel *Daily Cinema News*. [According to the writer of this article, *Daily Cinema News* was owned by Archie Mitchell and was the first and only newsreel to issue daily. However, I could find no trace of it. Was it perhaps a local reel? If any reader can supply information about it I should be grateful. Ed.]

94   ANON. 'Personality—the problem of commentary'. *World Film News*, vol. 1, no. 5 (August 1936), p.41.

The author, 'a well-known newsreel commentator', claims that the secret of real success in speaking commentaries is to create a personality—adopt a particular style suited to the voice, stick to it, 'without trying to be six different commentators rolled into one'. Outlines argument for having two or three commentators per reel, each voice associated with a particular type of story. Discusses briefly how the commentator should work with the editor in the writing of the commentary.

95   ANON. 'Newsreels analysis—July'. *World Film News*, vol. 1, no. 6 (September 1936), p.31.

A table of newsreel contents for July reveals that all five newsreels devote about 50% to the three stock subjects—sport, royalty and military. *British Movietone News* and *Gaumont-British News* had appreciably more foreign coverage than the others. 'While speed and efficiency of service to exhibitors have improved amazingly, it is not possible to say that there has been a corresponding improvement in the range and variety of news presented'.

96   SINCLAIR, A. W. F. 'Newsreel lacks drama, says editor of *Daily Sketch*'. *World Film News*, vol. 1, no. 6 (September 1936), p.31.

Interviewed by Denis Myers, A. W. F. Sinclair gives his opinions about the newsreels, e.g.: 'the newsreel makes the public more picture-minded; you can really speak of radio, newspaper and newsreel as a triumvirate of technology—the newspaper reflects life, the radio gives it atmosphere and the newsreel gives it animation; what the newsreel needs is dramatising—getting that human interest that it lacks at present; not only is one newsreel like its rival, it is so often a replica of any other week's issue; the public for newsreels is tremendous—they go from one news theatre to another . . . in a sort of newsreel pub-crawl; newsreel programmes need better balancing—beyond the cartoons there is too little that is light'.

97   CROSTHWAITE, Brian. 'Newsreels show political bias: editing of Spanish War Scenes discloses partisan views'. *World Film News*, vol. 1, no. 7 (October 1936), p.41.

Takes issue with the reporting of the Spanish Civil War, by the British newsreel companies in particular with 'The Blonde Amazon' story in issue number 274, 13 August 1936, of the Gaumont-British newsreel. Claims that 'in recent newsreel issues about Spain the pro-rebel bias has been too obvious to escape notice'.

98   CUMMINS, G. T. 'How they make up your newsreel . . .' *The Cinema*, (7 October 1936), p.xi, (Supplement).

Detailed article by the Editor of *British Paramount News* on the technical side of the planning, shooting and high-speed delivery of the Paramount reel. The company uses planes to take films to and from transatlantic liners. It records sound in the field: a non-directional microphone is now part of the standard equipment used by every sound man who 'produces' the story according to national and local requirements. Light-weight sound trucks are so designed that their entire equipment can be rapidly dismantled and re-erected in any desired location. The sound system is so arranged that adequate separation between the recording amplifier, camera and microphones is possible. New fully-automatic high-speed negative developing equipment has been added to existing laboratory facilities. Paramount's 'specially adapted editing machines' cut editing time to a minimum. The company's 'ultra-rapid printer' is capable of dealing with 240 feet of 35mm. film per minute and prints four complete copies of sound and picture simultaneously. An additional ten-gang printer, recently introduced, makes it possible to produce ten copies of the newsreel in the time normally required for one.

99   ANON. 'Newsreel rushes, by The Commentator'. *World Film News*, vol. 1, no. 8, (November 1936), p.38.

Speculates on the possibility of a merger involving Gaumont-British, Pathé Gazette and British Movietone. A brief item compliments Paramount for its 'fine newsreel reporting' of the blowing up of the Alcazar.

100   CUMMINS, G. T. 'Editors criticisms'. *World Film News*, vol. 1, no. 8 (November 1936), p.39.

Mr Cummins, the Editor of *Paramount British News*, claims that the 'larger part' of the editor's work is done 'long before a camera turns': the aspects of a story that the camera crew concentrates on is settled in advance. At times 'expert witnesses' are obtained 'to clarify and explain the significance of current events'.

101   ANON. 'Making and showing newsreels: N. J. Hulbert, M. P., wants better public control service: censorship and propaganda points raised in Merseyside lecture'. *Kinematograph Weekly*, (5 November 1936), p.17.

Reports at length an address by Norman Hulbert, MP., L.C.C., Managing Director of Capital and Provincial News Theatres Ltd., to the members of the Merseyside Film Institute Society at Liverpool, on the previous Friday, on 'The production and exhibition of news films'. Replying to questions afterwards Hulbert made a number of points: it was the editors of the newsreels who selected the politicians for the screen talks, and their selection depended on their news value at the time. Politicians were not paid by the newsreel companies, neither was any payment made to the latter. Anything of a general propaganda nature was selected on the basis of its news value ... the reason for the inclusion of a high proportion of military displays was that they were attractive items ... He went on: 'There is no censorship of newsreels and I hope there never will be because newsreels are talking newspapers'. There was no Government control, although sometimes a hint might be given that it is not desirable to publish a certain item, and it was usual to respect their wishes on such occasions.

102   ANON. 'Newsreel rushes by The Commentator'. *World Film News*, vol. 1, no. 9 (December 1936), p.40–41.

Among a number of items notes: 'An incredible blunder was made by all the newsreels in their issues dated November 9th; apparently suffering from a surfeit of "intelligent anticipation" they announced the fall of Madrid and some even included shots purporting to show the entry of Franco's troops into the City. The newsreels had entirely miscalculated the capacity of the Government forces to defend the Capital. This is not the first time that their information about Spain has been inaccurate and ill-informed. Maybe it will teach them a lesson'. The final item in the 'Rushes' reviews the Armistice Day specials of the five newsreels.

103   CALDER-MARSHALL, A. 'Propaganda in the films'. *Life and Letters To-day*, vol. 15, no. 6 (Winter 1936–37), p.151–61.

Defines propaganda as being of two types, static and dynamic. Static propaganda is employed by those in power, dynamic by those out of power. The former is easier to disguise than the latter because it is sedative. Dynamic propaganda is at a disdvantage. 'It has to offer for a known compost of good and evil a reorganisation of society which it believes to be superior, but which static propaganda has done its utmost to represent as ruin'. In this context, looks at feature film first, then goes on to take issue with statements made by John Grierson on propaganda and the documentary in particular with the assertion that 'if propaganda takes on its other more political meaning, the sooner documentary is done with it the better'. Then turns to propaganda and the news-films. Having seen most of the newsreels of the Spanish troubles the author has noticed the following facts about them: 'In no film was any explanation given of how the war arose, who started it and what the Government is fighting for. Shots were shown of churches in ruins and burnt out, but no explanation was given, except that of atheistic terrorism'. 'The cleverest piece of propaganda was the interview with the "Blonde Amazon"' ... It is not that news-films are consistently used by right wing propagandists to distort news or form public opinion. 'The present news-films are not made with any deliberate purpose'. However, where there is a propagandist bias that bias is to the right, 'the result perhaps as much of common stupidity as of political cunning'. Ends with a plea for the making of left-wing films dealing with contemporary events, in the first instance covering the situation in Spain and in Abyssinia.

104   GEMMELL, J. C. 'Standard of newsreels vastly improved'. *The Journal of the Association of Cine-Technicians',* (December 1936–January 1937), p.78.

Suggests there is a feeling that 'this commentary business is a little overdone': the important thing is to get the story on the *screen.* The use of improved sound recording techniques allied to the results obtained with exceptionally long lenses from 40 to 17 inch focus has rendered 'absurdly obvious' comments unnecessary.

105   HOLT, Paul. 'Newsreels should take chances' *The Journal of the Association of Cine-Technicians,* (December 1936–January 1937), p.80.

Praises the standard of newsreel camerawork in the U.K. but suggests that newsreel cameramen are afraid to take a chance of securing the 'best picture': the fault is not necessarily with the cameramen, more with the news editors who send the cameramen out to cover a story.

1937

106   GRIERSON, John. *'Report on the distribution of Empire films in Great Britain and of British films in the Dominions and India'* (1937?). John Grierson Archive, Document no. G4:4:10.

Pages 28, 36–42 and 49 of the Report (believed to be an Imperial Relations Trust paper) deal with news film. 'In order to find the representation of Empire countries in the British newsreels an examination has been made of the programmes distributed during the six months from 1st July to 31st December 1937 by four of the five news reel companies' (*Universal Talking News* were not prepared to supply the necessary information). The results of the analysis are tabled. 'The main conclusion which emerges is that, on the whole, Empire countries only appear at very infrequent intervals...' British news film items are much better represented in the Dominion cinemas than features or shorts. 'Most of the companies have agreements with Dominion news film distributors according to which British reels are shown either in their entirety, side by side with local reels, or else are largely embodied in the latter. Where the British news reel company is American controlled, however, it sometimes happens that the American, rather than the British, edition of the reel is sent to the Dominions. This seems to a large extent to be the case in Canada...'

107   WARREN, Low. *The Film Game.* London: T. Werner Laurie, 1937. xvi, 236p.

Chapter 17, 'How topical films are made: the cavalcade of topical events upon the screen—how news pictures are obtained—the rush to secure a "scoop"—by aeroplane and car—and what it means in terms of wear and tear—and courage—a showman who tried to scoop the pool with a topical—but "got the bird" instead', p.145–153, covers the above topics. Popular treatment.

108   ANON. 'Newsreel rushes by the Commentator' *World Film News,* vol. 1, no. 10 (January 1937), p.39.

Discusses the newsreel coverage of the Constitutional crisis over the abdication of King Edward VIII. Finds that 'with the entire British Press "ostriching", it was too much to expect the infinitely more cowardly newsreels to take an independent line'. Interest therefore centred on transatlantic reports. Concludes: 'So badly had the newsreels got the jitters over the Constitutional crisis that even when King Edward VIII abdicated, their specials were contemptible. None of them had the courage to face up to the issue involved and the attempt to use the Queen Mary angle plus stock shots of the new King to cover up their cowardice, impressed nobody. The crisis has clearly demonstrated that the newsreels are dependent upon and fearful of the magic word *authority* and that they are unable to fulfil their responsibilities to the public on an issue of domestic importance. When will one of the newsreels have the courage to breakthrough?'

109   MacDONALD, Alister G. 'Cameo News Theatre, Victoria Street, S.W.' *The Architect's Journal*, vol. 85 (7 January 1937), p.32–3.

Architectural diagrams, supplemented by photographs of the interior, of the Cameo News Theatre opposite Victoria Station (the entrance was in Victoria Street though the bulk of the site faces Allington Street), designed by MacDonald.

110   ANON. 'Newsreel rushes by The Commentator'. *World Film News*, vol. 1, no. 11 (February 1937), p.42–3.

Accords *Gaumont-British News* the accolade of being the year's best newsreel of 1936: E. V. H. Emmett's commentaries are complimented; exciting shots highlighted; unity of 'pull' between pictures, sound, music and commentary remarked upon. This approach is contrasted with *Movietone*'s 'measured, stately progress', and that newsreel's neglect of the best use of natural sound and its excessive commentary; with *Paramount*'s 'formal dullness' and its over-wordy and too speedily delivered commentaries; with *Universal*'s re-recording of all natural sound because that newsreel has no sound unit; with *Pathé Gazette*'s lack of any natural sound and its 'chronological mix-up', the latter a fault shared with *Paramount* and *Universal*. Concludes by advocating the *Gaumont-British News* system of production pointing out that G.B's lead is due to the fact that 'the entire make-up of the reel, the cutting, commentating and re-recording is under the control of the commentator Emmett'.

111   ANON. 'Newsreel rushes, by The Commentator'. *World Film News*, vol. 1, no. 12 (March 1937), p.37.

Considers the implications for the newsreels in the reports that the B.B.C. is soon to have available two television "Outside Broadcast" vans complete with Emitron cameras, under the headings, 'the importance of editing', 'the commercial aspect' and 'censorship'. It is felt that television editing will not be up to the standard of film editing. Claims that 'over 90 per cent of present day newsreel stories are based on the hope of publicity for someone or something': the organisers of sporting events are happy to allow the newsreel companies to screen highlights of the events after these have taken place: 'television will be the world's greatest box-office and turnstile killer' and the organisers' response to a request for the televising of 'a *whole* match to the *whole* country' can be easily imagined. Censorship in the official B.B.F.C. sense does not apply to the newsreels but 'censorship through the editor does exist'. Without stating why "The Commentator" insists that with television all such self-censorship will be impossible, 'leading' to many a newsreel story being barred from the viewing screen'. Concludes by suggesting that television may one day solve the newsreel's biggest problem—distribution.

112   ANON. 'Newsreel rushes, by The Commentator'. *World Film News*, vol. 2, no. 1 (April 1937), p.28.

Among the topics briefly referred to in this number of the regular column are 1) the takeover of *Gaumont-British News* by C. M. Woolf's General Film Distributors which already owned *Universal News* and 2) arrangements for the newsreel coverage of the Coronation, including the censoring of all reels by the Archbishop of Canterbury and the Earl Marshall.

113   ANON. 'Newsreel rushes, by The Commentator'. *World Film News*, vol. 2, no. 2 (May 1937), p.3.

Outlines arrangements for the newsreel coverage of the Coronation—*Movietone* to film in colour and in black and white; *Pathé* and *Movietone* to film the events inside Westminster Abbey, the pictures to be shared with the other reels; *Paramount* to have 50 cameramen covering the event exposing 25,000 feet of stock, *Movietone* to expose 40,000 feet; *Gaumont-British News* and *Universal* promise to expose over one million feet *each*! etc.

114   ANON. 'Diary of the Coronation reels'. *World Film News*, vol. 2, no. 3 (June 1937), p.19.

Comments on the newsreel coverage of the Coronation. At the last moment the Earl Marshall had found room for all five newsreels to film the Service in the Abbey and had given greatly increased facilities to the cameramen. All five reels were to exchange rota prints. About 10,000 feet of film exposed within the Abbey. It was felt that Pathé had produced the best version of the story.

115   ANON. 'Newsreel rushes, by The Commentator'. *World Film News*, vol. 2, no. 3 (June 1937), p.31.

Discusses the disadvantages of the Royal rota system at length. Briefly compliments *Gaumont-British* for a 'superbly edited story on wiped out Guernica'; laments a 'staggering mishandling' of the bus strike by all five newsreels and accuses the reels of having been 'afraid' of the topic. Enquiries about the identity of 'The Commentator' answered: WFN's newsreel material, 'much of which is exclusive information, is received from several authoritative sources and edited by Raymond East'.

116   ANON. 'Duke of Windsor's wedding films banned in Britain by "agreement": English newsreel executives accede to "suggestions" that exhibition would not interest public: reels rushed to U.S.' *Motion Picture Herald*, (12 June 1937), p.54.

The American journal reports that the newsreel film of the wedding reached American theatres after a transatlantic race against time which rivalled that staged for the Coronation pictures, but that audiences in England and the Dominions, 'closer to if not more interested in the event than the rest of the world', would not see them. An Associated Press dispatch said that the British newsreel executives were said to have been led to believe that as the British public was still so enraptured with the Coronation of Edward's successor they would not care for pictures of the Duke's wedding. The 'Daily Express', the only London paper to comment on the decision informed its readers: 'You will have to go to France or America—or maybe Russia—to see them, thereby proving that, though a large-sized piece of humbug is talked over here about freedom from censorship and from what not, the Imperial British people are still treated as a mentally deficient race'. Gerald Sanger, spokesman for the English newsreels, explained: 'It was felt that to release films of the wedding might reawaken painful emotions and even lead to invidious demonstrations in the theatres'. Anyway, Mr Sanger said, the pictures were not so good. 'They were merely animated facsimiles of the photographs that appeared in the press'. The United Press reported that the newsreel companies had received strong but indirect hints from official quarters that it would be 'good policy' not to include pictures of the wedding in releases for the Empire. (There is a brief introductory note about the affair on page 8.)

117   ANON. 'Newsreel rushes by The Commentator'. *World Film News*, vol. 2, no. 4 (July 1937), p.29.

Under the sub-heading 'Historic Mistakes' quotes John Grierson's comment in an earlier issue of *World Film News*: 'The newsreel . . . is rushing breathlessly to oblivion'. Takes the newsreels to task for their non-coverage over the past year of labour disturbances and the abdication and for 'their failure to please renter, exhibitor or public over the Coronation'. Goes on: 'World events of the past year seemed to have conspired to show up the British newsreels at their most cowardly, most incompetent'. Under the sub-heading, 'Case History of a Failure' writes: 'On May 25th, four men walked into the shining new offices of British Movietonews in London's Soho Square. They were: R. S. Howard, Editor of *Gaumont-British News*; Cecil Snape of Universal, Louis Behr of Pathé; and G. T. Cummins of Paramount. Inside, they were met by Gerald Sanger, Movietone's Production Chief, for a hush-hush heart-to-heart. Within a few minutes they had reached complete agreement. The Wedding of the Duke of Windsor was *BARRED* from every screen in Britain. Britain's cinema addicts had lost the year's biggest story after the Coronation. The trade had lost the chance to pack every movie house in the country solid, for days on end. So quickly did the newsreel's "big five" make their decision, that at first there were rumours of hands being forced by Government pressure or interference from powerful vested interests. Later information showed that they had acted entirely off their own bat. What underlying reasons led to the anti-Windsor policy? The newsreels' official statement that "they were respecting the Duke of Windsor's desire for privacy" was plainly ridiculous, when every newspaper was screaming headlines round the world...' Another item in the 'Rushes' refers to the newsreels' use of lenses with focal lengths of 40, 50 and 56 inches.

118   ANON. 'Sound City to launch news reel: *National News* to start in October'. *To-day's Cinema*, (6 July 1937), p.1.

Norman Loudon of Sound City announces that another national newsreel is to be launched in October. Production will be in the hands of Cecil R. Snape (formerly of *Universal Talking News*). Executive Manager will be Victor Creer. Many novel features and events not usually covered by newsreels will be introduced. *National News* will have the advantage of close association with Messrs. George Humphries & Co., the well-known film printers. Experts in every department of newsreel production are already recruited.

119   NORRIS, Glen. 'A wide open letter to Mr G. T. Cummins... Editor of *British Paramount News*'. *World Film News*, vol. 2, no. 5 (August 1937), p.30–1.

A special item in the 'Newsreel rushes' column, 'the first of a series of articles in which (the) contributor submits the British newsreels to candid and constructive criticism'. Norris writes that each of the five British newsreels has its own flavour—each is stamped with the personality of its commentators and cutters and above all its editor. After pointing out that camerawork is the outstanding feature of *British Paramount News*, and that this reel often scoops the others because of its efficient, world-wide network for collecting and transporting film, he then embarks on a detailed criticism of the reel. The basic problem is that the reel is not fast enough and the solution is more speed and less repetition. Cutting shows signs of 'old silent style'. Continuity 'sustaining' shots should be omitted and their message left to the commentator. Reel uses two commentators: the addition of a third for comedy and a fourth for 'big' drama would help. Reform needed in the writing of the commentaries—too often the obvious is pointed out. Finally, more music should be used.

120   ANON. 'Newsreel rushes: notes by The Commentator'. *World Film News*, vol. 2, no. 5 (August 1937), p.31.

Under the sub-heading 'Frightful film', the writer describes how Orlando Lippert of U.S. *Paramount News* covered the Chicago steel riots. The negative showed police brutality so clearly it was immediately confiscated by the U.S. Government. 'A few of the less harrowing shots' were released in the U.K. by *British Paramount News* (issue no. 656, 10 June 1937). When the Paramount pictures formed evidence at the strike enquiry *British Paramount News* released a second story in issue no. 659, 21 June 1937.

121   ANON. 'Newsreel rushes: notes by The Commentator'. *World Film News*, vol. 2, no. 5, (August 1937), p.31.

Brief item on setting up of a new newsreel, *National News*, to be edited by the longtime *Universal News* editor, Cecil R. Snape and to be under the financial control of the Sound City studio group, headed by Norman Loudon. *National News* is to have its own fleet of sound tracks. Snape to edit for first time using natural sound as *Universal News* did not have this facility.

Chicago riots—see abstract 120 (courtesy of the National Film Archive)

122   ANON. 'News of the quarter: China war newsreels'. *Sight & Sound*, vol. 6, no. 23 (Autumn 1937), p.116.

Comments on the 'considerable controversy' provoked by the horrific newsreel material from Shanghai issued in *British Paramount News* and *Universal Talking News*. Quotes Jeffrey Bernerd, head of *Gaumont-British News* and the *Daily Film Renter* editorial. Concludes: 'It is impossible to say "what the public thought" but ordinary cinema managers and news theatre managers reported little complaint and much approval'.

123   SETON, Marie. 'The British Cinema 1914'. *Sight & Sound*, vol. 6, no. 23 (Autumn 1937), p.126–28.

In this article, the third of a series on the history of the British film industry from 1896 to 1937 the author illustrates from the film trade press, in effect *The Bioscope*, what happened between August and December 1914. 'After the defeat of the Boers the British cinema industry stored away its potentialities of direct propaganda until England was again embroiled in war. But during the intervening years the status of the film had so risen that its value was recognised by the most august bodies'. Quotes debate on matters of censorship, especially of war film news, and the introduction of the Trading with the Enemy Act. The film trade had other urgent problems: how would a prolonged war affect audiences and what films would they want?

124   NORRIS, Glen. 'A wide-open letter to Mr Gerald Sanger, Production Chief of British Movietonews'. *World Film News*, vol. 2, no. 6 (September 1937), p.32–3.

First lists advantages of *British Movietone News*: lavish equipment and staff; backed by enormous resources of Movietonews of America which in turn is funded by Twentieth Century Fox; uses several commentators; has good titling (but could be improved); groups news stories under general headings. Disadvantages: the American parent company lends its worldwide network of staff cameramen but also largely controls production policy of the British reel; while in the U.S. the voice of each commentator has its own distinct and immediately recognisable personality, in Britain voices are average posh, no one instantly recognisable; stories are dull, padded with foolish jokes; the British reel sticks to the old fashioned system of writing commentaries to fit previously cut pictures instead of adopting the American technique of using a fast moving commentary illustrated by exciting shots. Solutions to lack of speed in *British Movietone News*, 1) adopt a more unified control over the various production departments and 2) find a place in the organisation for one man who would combine something of the work of a chief cutter with that of a scriptwriter.

125   ANON. 'Wardour Street gossip by "Tatler"'. *Daily Film Renter*, (14 September 1937), p.2.

A brief item in the column refers to the scenes of the Japanese-Chinese war in the current issue of *Universal Talking News*. The columnist feels 'unhesitatingly' that they ought to be shown and writes: 'Personally, I think it is time news reels showed the public these terrors and horrors, so that people themselves can see that it's no drawing-room entertainment but stark realism in all its grimmest and most horrible truth'.

126   ANON. 'News reels give anti-war lead: the real facts from Shanghai battlefields: courageous national service by screen editor: a lesson for the public'. *To-day's Cinema*, (14 September 1937), p.1, 11.

Begins: 'This week several of the newsreels achieve a new importance in national service. They have decided to show the public the truth about war'. Quotes G. T. Cummins, Editor of *British Paramount News*, 'It is our duty to give the news. These things are happening, and we have decided to show them. The only way to stop war is to give people a proper idea of what it means'. Cummins holds that it is a duty of the newsreel to take its part in awakening the conscience of the world. Paramount issued the following statement: 'Nothing more grim than these pictures could possibly be shown on the screen, but as the Paramount commentator observes, the task of a newsreel in reporting a war is to show the war as it is, rather than as a glorious pageant of embattled chivalry. The pictures show the results of the use of high explosives against civilians; they are the only actual pictures. Trimming or faking was out of the question. Either they had to be shown as they were or suppressed. Few will quarrel with Paramount's decision to release them'. Paramount prefaced these shots with a warning caption to the audience announcing what was about to be shown, so that those members of an audience who wished could refrain from seeing it.

127   ANON. 'Shanghai film disagreement: Mr Jeffrey Bernerd on newsreel policy: arguments against horrors: "protecting" exhibitors'. *The Cinema*, (15 September 1937), p.3, 47.

Bernerd, Gaumont-British newsreel chief in a statement to *The Cinema* takes the strongest issue with the editors of the other reels who have decided to show the Shanghai battles in their full grimness: 'It is the duty of the newsreels to present news, but not to put on the screen material for a political purpose ... exhibitors of this country run their theatres with the idea of entertaining their public. The public trust exhibitors to show entertainment, and therefore they take their children ... To show the ghastly destruction of human beings in the most horrific form is, I contend, letting down the exhibitor ... By all means show pictures of the Shanghai bombardment to Chamberlain, Hitler, Mussolini, Roosevelt, and other leaders. They should see them; but not the people in the picture houses that pay their sixpence or ninepence to be entertained'.

128   ANON. 'Newsreel policy on war: Mr G. T. Cummins replies to Mr Bernerd: "20th Century phenomenon": right to report in pictures'. *To-day's Cinema*, (17 September 1937), p.1, 8.

'Newsreel chiefs are at variance over the proper function of a newsreel'. Cummins states: 'To me, the newsreel [is] a phenomenon of the twentieth century, which deserves greater intelligence than as a medium for the presentation of mediocre pictures of laying of foundation stones or seaside baby shows solely for the purpose of scoring with an effective wisecrack. The newsreel deserves the position which it can achieve of being a worthy screen representative of the Fourth Estate reporting with equal freedom and as much intelligence the trends and events of this amazing world in which we live'. Contrary to Mr Bernerd's expectations 'managers are reporting that on every hand is heard the point of view that "every adult should be forced to see this . . . it would stop a lot of this cheap talk of war".'

129   *To-day's Cinema*. Leading article. 'An open letter to Mr G. T. Cummins, Editor of *British Paramount News*'. (17 September 1937), p.6.

Discusses Cummins's decision to include in his newsreels 'scenes showing the true meaning of modern warfare'. *To-day's Cinema* finds itself 'to some extent on both sides' of the argument. It agrees entirely that 'newsreels should have the same degree of "journalistic" freedom as is accorded to the Press'. Against the presentation of 'the whole truth and nothing but the truth' in newsreels is the fact that these are usually available in all programmes and children see them. 'This argument of the children is not an argument against including definitely "adult" subjects in newsreels, but against letting the children in to see them unwarned'. However, as it is the case that when the company sends out its reels it informs the exhibitors of the nature of their contents this entirely meets the objection. The responsibility for the matter thus rests with the exhibitor 'upon whom devolves the duty either of expunging the items under discussion, or of warning his patrons about what they are going to see'.

130   ANON. 'Newsreel rushes: newsreel notes by The Commentator'. *World Film News*, vol. 2, no. 7 (October 1937), p.35.

Reviews the organisation behind the new newsreel *National News*, the first issue of which is to appear the same month. Man behind the venture is Norman Loudon, Chairman of the production and distribution company, Sound City Ltd. Editor Cecil R. Snape comes from *Universal News*, with the experience of having personally supervised the production of more than 25,000 newsreel stories. Commentator is ex-BBC Thomas Woodroffe. Cameramen are Eric Owen and J. Humphries from *Gaumont-British News*, Jerry Somers and S. Swan from *Universal News* and S. Bartholomew, a free-lancer with *Pathé Gazette*. Sound team to be headed by Leslie Murray and F. Ralph of *British Movietone News*. Distribution through Sound City Distributors. New features promised for the new reel include printing in three different lengths, presenting five star (12,000 feet), four star (800 feet) and three star (500 feet) editions instead of the standard 850 feet issue; making up the reel with a smaller number of bigger stories and commentating in the fast-moving American style. The commentator is to collaborate in the writing of scripts for stories before they are shot and is to work in close co-operation with the editor and cutters.

131   ANON. '*National News* makes its debut: three special features: colour, cartoon and history behind the news: aims and policy'. *Daily Film Renter*, (12 October 1937), p.7.

Introduces with illustrations the directors and staff of the new company, outlines its policy and describes some of the technical equipment the company will be using. Pages 5–11 contain further information and advertisements (including congratulatory ones from processing firms and suppliers).

132   *Daily Film Renter*. Leading article. 'The real trouble'. (12 October 1937), p.2.

Reports that in future the Northern Ireland Government will ban all films dealing with Irish problems following the calling in of the police during the showing of the film 'Beloved Enemy' in Belfast. 'The Emerald Isle is not the only place where strife and commotion is caused by the showing of pictures which upset the equanimity of certain patrons' political opinions. A West End news reel theatre was the scene of a fracas between Chinese and Japanese recently. The kinema is certainly no place for propaganda'.

133   ANON. '*National News* launched: features of individuality: section in Dunning colour: cartoon on current events: personnel behind new enterprise'. *The Cinema* (13 October 1937), p.19.

Introduces with illustrations the directors and staff of the new company, outlines its policy and describes some of the technical equipment the company will be using. Pages 17–23 contain further information and advertisements (including congratulatory ones from processing firms and suppliers). The company's logo on page 17 shows a bulldog's head staring straight at the viewer, surrounded by a laurel wreath with the words 'National News' in 'Old English' letters underneath and above the wreath the words 'Here, There and Everywhere'.

134   ANON. '*National News* calls a halt: withdrawn from circulation for time being: to raise standard: surprise pause on part of News Reel'. *To-day's Cinema* (14 October 1937), p.1.

This announcement was made by the new company the day previously. 'Having set themselves only to present the best, the directors of *National News* are temporarily withdrawing *National News* from circulation until the standard they present is consistent with the high level they have announced. This pause will only be a short one and will give time for the complete installation of equipment which is still awaiting delivery'.

135   ANON. 'Newsreel rushes: newsreel notes by The Commentator'. *World Film News*, vol. 2, no. 8 (November 1937), p.37.

Reviews the reception of the *National News* which was born on 11th October and which 'was dead of a broken heart' on October 13th. Further features promised for the reel had been the provision of a regular section in colour (for the first time in any newsreel) and a regular section of 'news behind the headlines' in the style of *The March of Time*. The almost unanimous verdict of the few thousands who saw the first reel during the two days that it was showing was that it was terribly disappointing. The finished product was rated slipshod, unimaginative, lacking both news and entertainment value. The colour quality of the colour section was bad and the choice of an army mannequin parade of uniforms, which might have been shot months earlier, for the first colour story was another bad start. Commentator Woodroffe failed to adapt his radio technique to the lighter, more concentrated newsreel style.

136   ANON. 'Newsreel rushes: newsreel notes by The Commentator'. *World Film News*, vol. 2, no. 8 (November 1937), p.37.

Brief items compliment *British Paramount News* on some recent stories, e.g. the 'uncensored pictures of the Shanghai bombing horror', and in particular for scooping all its rivals by being the only newsreel to send cameramen to cover Sir Oswald Mosley taking his fascists down to London's East End again on October 10th when there was renewed rioting.

137   ANON. 'What children prefer on the screen: analysis of questionnaire to Odeon Managers: action films liked best: views on programme length, newsreels and stars'. *Kinematograph Weekly*, (3 November 1938), p.1.

Children's likes and dislikes in film fare, the views of 151,000 children are set out in a summary issued by Odeon Theatres as a result of a questionnaire to managers. The ages of children range from three and five years to eleven and fourteen. 'In newsreels, which are usually welcomed with hand-clapping, royalty scenes are most loudly cheered (61 per cent), military and naval scenes are second (32 per cent), sports items are third (30 per cent). Foreign dictators come in for the loudest boo of disapproval, 53 per cent being the estimated dislike'.

138   ANON. 'Newsreel rushes: newsreel notes by The Commentator'. *World Film News*, vol. 2, no. 9 (December 1937), p.39.

Discusses commentating and contrasts British and American styles. U.S. *Paramount News* had just reversed its policy of maintaining complete anonymity for its commentators, a policy which *British Paramount News* also shared. No change as yet at the British reel but as the American parent company keeps a tight hold on its British Branch the possibility exists that *British Paramount News* may soon name its two mystery voices. Assesses the well-known British commentators, E. V. H. Emmett of *Gaumont-British News*, R. E. Jeffrey of *Universal News*, Roy de Groot of *Pathé Gazette* and the *British Movietone News* team headed by Sir Malcolm Campbell (who makes only rare appearances), Eric Dunstan, Leslie Mitchell, Ivan Scott, Alan Howland and Beryl de Querton ('Britain's only regular commentatrice'). Each of these 'voices of Britain' is heard by an average of about fifteen million cinemagoers a week.

139   GRINLEY, Charles. 'Notes on the news-reel'. *Life and Letters Today*, vol. 17, no. 10 (Winter 1937), p.122–8.

Gives some examples to make the point that the public has 'become used to news-reels being deleted or doctored'. Even in the early days of the news-reels the format and make-up which militated against the true reporting of news was evident. 'True news-reporting does not consist only of presenting facts. It consists of presenting them so that they make their full impression. In a reel of five items, you can present appalling shots of an earthquake. But you can make it seem unimportant, even irrelevant, by glossing it over and surrounding it with four others of say, a cricket match, Ascot, a ceremonial parade, a royal drive'. Editors do not fulfil their responsibilities as journalists as do newspaper editors. The reason there is not much variety in the reels lies in the 'picture people's idea of the audience'. The news-reel's political or propagandist aspect is patent. 'Certain reels are under the control of those from whom unbiassed views is hardly to be expected . . . Now that the news-reel is news, it is essential that it should wake up to the sense of duty which has, believe it or not, animated the better sections of the press'. For all its apparent 'service' the newsreel is not giving 'the real news'. In consequence, audiences do not give the newsreel the whole of their attention. 'They drop in, notice the items they want, doze through the rest. They don't study how it is put together or what outlook it expresses. And so, by degrees, slogans can be dinned into the audiences' ears till they become familiar with them, the first step toward accepting them. A viewpoint can be presented until it seems the natural one. Subtly, the propaganda of the news-reel can sink in—without anyone asking whose propaganda it is'.

140   SETON, Marie. 'War'. *Sight & Sound*, vol. 6, no. 24 (Winter 1937–38), p.182–85.

In this article, the fourth of a series on the history of the British film industry from 1896 to 1937 the author looks at film in war-time, illustrating her article with quotations from the daily press. Discusses the reception of "The Battle of the Somme", then turns to the newsreel. 'Go anywhere, anytime, anyhow and get home' was the motto of the *Pathé Gazette* quintette of cameramen. Unlike the French cameramen at the front the British, although they were given Army rank, had no military training. 'The general opinion, expressed by both official War Office cameramen and independent newsreel men, is that British audiences did not have the same taste for gruesome pictures as the Continent, an attitude of mind which has persisted'. Cameramen found that they were given every facility in France. Frank Basil, one of the Pathé cameramen felt that the newsreel man's job was no more difficult during war than in peace-time—providing he did not mind the risks. Restrictions based on pre-war customs began to be modified. Interviewing important people became increasingly easy.

1938

141   HUMPHREY, Robert. *Careers in the films*. London: Pitman, 1938, 104p.

Chapter 7, 'The news-reel cameraman', p.69–76, describes the work of the professional cameraman and gives the qualities he needs—'a thick skin, indomitable push, and boundless ingenuity and resource to help him in the tight corners in which he will inevitably find himself; and, most important of all, plenty of tact and patience to deal with all sorts of authorities, both reasonable and unreasonable . . . the ability to make a quick decision is essential, as also is a certain flair for what is of news interest'.

142   ANON. 'R. E. Jeffrey back from Spain: Franco poses for pictures: front line trench experiences: operator's narrow escape from snipers: 2,000 feet film record secured'. *To-day's Cinema*, (12 February 1938), p.1, 4.

Outlines the experiences of Jeffrey, the *Universal Talking News* commentator and his cameraman, George Oswald, during a fortnight's visit to insurgent Spain. Asked for his reason in undertaking the trip Jeffrey replied: 'For a long time I have been dissatisfied with just adding a commentary to what is sent in. After this visit I am able to speak with authority of what I have seen. Newsreels should be able to take a better place in journalism than just being subjects for amusement'.

143   BUTLER, Richard. 'Newsreel man in the firing line: the adventures and misadventures of Richard Butler, Pathé cameraman in search of newsreel pictures on the Aragon front'. *World Film News* vol. 2, no. 12 (March 1938), p.6–8.

The cameraman reported first to British Consulate in Barcelona and was advised to get out of Spain without delay as it was not considered safe for him to attempt to photograph. Then visited Commission of Propaganda, F.A.I. Headquarters, and P.O.U.M. seeking permission to photograph. Propaganda people eventually arranged papers for him and he set off for the Aragon front. Took shots of snipers, dead Moors and trenches. No photographs were allowed to be taken of guns or the activities of gunners. Front line kitchens visited. Took shots of an attack by Government troops through a rifle firing hole. Visited Huesca front line. Had cameras and films confiscated at one point. Eventually got cameras back but films went to Madrid to be developed and censored from whence they were to be sent on to the Commission for Propaganda in Barcelona. Just before leaving for England he learned that the films in question would be shown to the various censor committees, who, if they considered it prudent to release the films, would instruct the Commission of Propaganda to have them dispatched via express to Paris. The censorship problem was his biggest 'headache'.

144   ANON. 'News-reels dilemma: problems of political reporting: manager's criticism'. *To-day's Cinema*, (1 March 1938), p.1.

Quotes P. W. Dennis, Manager of the Tatler News Theatre in Chester who in a letter to the Press had criticised the attitude of newsreels in handling major political events. Referring to the Eden resignation Dennis had written: 'Cinema audiences, allowed in the Press to read forthright expressions of opinion on the rights and wrongs of the case, have been treated by the news-reel companies to the baldest statement of the facts coupled with some shots of the leading characters. In some cases even this "bald and unconvincing narrative" was delayed three days before issue, possibly in the hope that something might turn up which would relieve the embarrassment of the commentators, who have withheld comment which may freely be expressed in any newspaper's leading articles and which is being amply and audibly expressed in the cinemas by the public themselves. This "hush hush" reporting was true of all but one firm, which was so "indiscreet" as to allow a prominent critic of the Government to speak his views to the camera. Within a couple of hours of delivery of this reel to the exhibitors urgent orders were issued that the item must be deleted. Unless our news-reels are allowed the liberty of expression on matters of political and other importance that is accorded to the Press we shall be doomed to a succession of inarticulate reports of bare facts, valueless cinematically and valueless as screen journalism, in a country where the liberty of journalism stands high'.

145   *To-day's Cinema*. Leading article. 'An open letter to Mr P. W. Dennis, Manager of the Tatler News Theatre, Chester'. (1 March 1938), p.5.

Begins, in reply to Mr Dennis's letter to the Press, 'Dear Showman,—We can't agree with you'. Goes on: 'The problem facing the newsreels is very different from that of the Press. Most organs of the National Press are frankly partisan to one policy or the other, and their politics are well known to their readers . . . But with a newsreel the problem is fundamentally different. An audience in any cinema includes all shades of political thought, from Communism to Fascism, and for any newsreel commentator to express a view on the rights and wrongs of any particular item is obviously liable to cause trouble. At least it will cause offence . . . We think the duty of the news-reel is to preserve complete impartiality, so far as is humanly possible . . . If newsreels are to commence to comment on the rights and wrongs of any political event, it will inevitably mean dividing cinemas into political categories—a result which would be disastrous to the box-office. The very fact, as you say, that comments on certain events are being "amply and audibly expressed in the cinemas by the public themselves" proves our point'.

146   ANON. 'Franco interview echo: "held balance as neutral": Mr R. E. Jeffrey's disclaimer: letter to exhibitor'. *The Cinema* (2 March 1938), p.50.

Reproduces part of a letter which Jeffrey, commentator for *Universal Talking News*, had sent to an exhibitor who announced his intention of terminating his contract for the screening of that newsreel in consequence of its inclusion of the pictures which the commentator had brought back from insurgent Spain. (Jeffrey had sent *To-day's Cinema* a copy of the letter.) Jeffrey writes that he is sorry that the exhibitor has not seen issue no. 794 for himself and that whoever told the exhibitor that he had been a guest of General Franco was 'very wide of his facts'. His employer, British Pictorial Productions Ltd. had paid his expenses. He had approached both sides in Spain but 'repeated applications to the Spanish embassy' brought him no encouragement to visit the Government side: after many attempts he secured a safe conduct to go into Nationalist Spain. Quotes part of his commentary, then goes on: 'In the whole of my commentary, apart from that quoted, I have held the balance as an absolute neutral, favouring neither side; and I challenge any impartial person or persons to dispute this. Possibly you may have noticed that the trade papers gave me credit for my neutral attitude in the matter. I claim that the showing of pictures of General Franco was *news*, as no one had been able to secure a camera interview with wife and family before, although many have attempted it'.

147   GRIERSON, John. 'Propaganda for democracy'. *The Spectator*, (11 November 1938), p.799–800.

Discusses the film picture of Britain that he would like to see at the New York World Fair in the spring of 1939. The Chairman of the Joint Committee of the British Council for Cultural Relations Abroad, Philip Guedalla has expressed himself as specially interested in a newsreel presentation of Britain and, in fact, the newsreels are the only section of the film industry on his committee. Grierson comments: 'Appreciating the news-reel presentation of Britain during the past few weeks, and, in particular, their shallow picture of Britain's social and political disposition to-day, one's doubts increase'.

148   MANDER, G. Le. 'Censorship and restriction of liberty'. Speech to House of Commons. *Hansard*, vol. 342 (28 November–22 December 1938), p.1262–77.

On the 7th of December Mr Mander moved: 'That this House, attaching the utmost importance to the maintenance undiminished of British democratic traditions in the liberty of expression of opinion, both in the Press and in public meetings and also in other media such as cinema films, would greatly deplore any action by the Government of the day which tended to set up any form of political censorship or which exercised pressure direct or indirect'. On page 1270 he turns to the newsreels, 'a very important new medium'. Gives examples of documentary and cinemagazine films that had been banned by the British Board of Film Censors and comments: 'I will ask the House to observe that in all these examples which I have given, in every case where cuts have been made nothing anti-Government, nothing anti-Fascist, is permitted, but anything that is favourable to the policy that the Government are pursuing is allowed to go forward. I venture to say that it is not the job of the British Board of Film Censors to deal with political matters of this kind at all'. Quotes a resolution sent him by the News Theatres Association: 'News Theatres in association have instructed me (that is, the Secretary) to say that they would resist by every legitimate means within their power the censorship of the news reel, or other screen news, which some might desire to impose—either officially or unofficially, from outside or inside the industry . . .' Then, relating to coverage of Czechoslovakian events he raises at length the matter of the *British Paramount News* issue of 21 September from which exhibitors were instructed by Paramount in answer to an official request to delete the speeches of Wickham Steed and A. J. Cummings. [Mr Mander had raised this matter at Question Time on 23 November—*Hansard*, vol. 341; 8 November–25 November 1938, p.1727–28 and, again on 1 December—*Hansard*, vol. 342; 28 November–22 December 1938, p.583.]

1939

149   SANGER, Gerald F. 'Freedom for the newsreel! We must fight any form of political censorship'. *Kinematograph Weekly*, (12 January 1939), p.45.

The Producer of *British Movietone News* notes that 'the veiled threat of the censorship of newsreels has again cropped up with varying intensity'. There are several forces ready to take advantage of any false step by any one of the newsreel companies to assail the whole status of the newsreel business—e.g. 'the believer in a more centralised, nationalised publicity' or 'municipal authorities with strong party leanings'. The Freedom of the Newsreel is a principle well established by now but it is not an absolute and arbitrary thing. 'It recognises certain practical limitations. For instance, no newsreel will issue a subject dealing with crime. This is a self-imposed ordinance. In the same way, newsreels avoid controversial subjects . . . In fact, the Freedom of the Newsreel rides along with its impartiality. And as newsreels have enshrined the principle of impartiality, so they claim to interpret it in their own way according to the traditions of free and unfettered Democratic Journalism.

150   ELVIN, George H. 'This freedom: an enquiry into film censorship'. *The Cine-Technician: the Journal of the Association of Cine-Technicians*, vol. 4, no. 19 (January-February 1939), p.141–46.

The article by the General Secretary of the Association of Cine-Technicians raises points about film censorship in general which affect the growth, power and prestige of the film industry. A paragraph on page 145 deals specifically with the newsreels: claims, and gives examples, that while the censor has no control over the newsreels, it is obvious that indirectly, if not directly, very great pressure is at times exercised. States, further, that part of the trouble is with the newsreel companies themselves because as the majority of their executives are government supporters, their newsreels naturally tend to reflect that fact. Tells the newsreel companies to remember that they are *news* reels and not propaganda sheets.

151   BLAKE, George. 'Magna it fama, or the rivalry between Newsreels, Newspapers, Radio and Television . . .' *Sight & Sound*, vol. 8, no. 29 (Spring 1939), p.10–11.

The newsreel cameraman's chief battle is for his position of vantage. Once there, it is a business of getting the focus and the exposure right and the cameraman has the machinery to help him do that. The broadcast commentator is in a much more vulnerable position.

152   ANON. 'Censored'. *The Cine-Technician: the Journal of the Association of Cine Technicians*, vol. 4, no. 20 (March-April 1939), p.202–204.

Responses to George H. Elvin's article on film censorship in the January-February issue, some of which refer specifically to the newsreels. A. J. Cummings of the *News Chronicle* cites as an example of Government pressure (repeating Elvin) the ignoring of the return from Spain of the British Battalion of the International Brigade which newspapers had covered in full and states that 'a few more instances of this kind of distortion of news values through political prejudices and the newsreel companies will entirely lose their popular appeal'. Geoffrey Mander, M.P. accuses the newsreels of pro-fascist bias. Clement J. Bundock, General Secretary of the National Union of Journalists raises the question of the 'suppression of inconvenient criticism'. Ronald Kidd, Secretary of the National Council of Civil Liberties refers to 'the steady development of a totalitarian frame of mind'. Ernest W. Fredman, Managing Editor, *Daily Film Renter*, stresses that it is most important that the 'screen remains free from *political* influence'.

153   NEILL-BROWN, J. 'The industry's front page news'. *The Cine-Technician: the Journal of the Association of Cine-Technicians*, vol. 4, no. 20 (March-April 1939), p.199–200.

Discusses the newsreel cinemas. There are about 22 of these small 300 to 500 seater halls in the country, 16 of them in London, all planned on more or less the same principle: in most of them the news only takes up short of twenty minutes of the hour's program but that twenty minutes forms the most important item of the program. Describes the audiences for these programs. Cinema managers say that 'they can frequently tell the political opinions of a commentator by the enthusiasm he displays'. Some managers would like their reels to be a 'little controversial', others tend to want 'to avoid any political slant whatsoever'. The latter usually make up their own reels from bits and pieces of others, taking good care to include only the sections that are likely to give no offence to any section of the audience, their policy being to do nothing that would antagonise the Government in power in case their actions should bring 'a stringent censorship' to bear on the newsreels. Finally discusses the type of programmes screened at the three West End news cinemas, the "Tatler", the "G.B. Movietone" (which claims to be the only genuine news theatre in London as it shows nothing else but news, except for a travel film now and then) and the "Cameo".

154   STAMP, Reginald. 'Local Authority and C.E.A. axis urged: friendly relations vital for kinema regulation'. *Kinematograph Weekly*, (29 June 1939), p.7.

The author, Chairman of the Entertainments Committee of the L.C.C., under a section headed 'Political interference', writes on the question of whether there is any direct official or political interference with the newsreels: . . . 'I desire it to be clearly understood that, while I am acting as custodian of the Cinematograph Act for such an important body as the L.C.C., I am not prepared to acquiesce in a situation that permits of interference, either by the withdrawal or re-editing, or special exclusion of particular films at request, or to eliminate certain features or part of them for political ends when the subjects are not in the nature of partisan politics. Such a situation can only end in local licensing authorities calling for censorship of newsreels, and in this matter I shall not be behind in taking the necessary initiative . . .'

155   MONTAGUE, W. P. *Letter to John Grierson* (9 October 1939), 7p. John Grierson Archive, Document no. G3:15:127.

The Assignment Editor of the American *Paramount News* writes to Grierson, c/o The British Embassy, Washington, D.C.: 'As you know, the newsreels try to be impartial on any job; they try to run both sides of any controversial subject and maintain the balance of both sides in effectiveness. The same goes as much for a war that we are not in as for a local political campaign. However, when it comes to the present war we are simply at our wits end to do a fair job, largely because of the unorganized and ineffective program that England and France have for newsreel coverage'. The newsreel material from England has been 'so weak as to be practically useless'. Complains that there is a lack of newsreel material 'from the allied side'; what there is is limited in scope or lacks interest. He is 'just not getting film from England' and has no way of knowing whether this is due to shortage of man power or censorship. In the first month of the war he received practically two shipments from Germany for every one from England. Outlines the range of subjects that could be shot in England and points out that to show the British Empire at war there must also be material from the colonies and dominions. What is coming from England is 'composed of trivialities' at a time when 'the best war newsreel pictures that have ever been made' are coming from Germany . . . 'Not only are they the best but they are cleverly planned'. At present the British censorship seems to be of a negative nature. Gives an example of good propaganda by the English censors to highlight even more negative attitudes in 'other parts of the Empire'. In Canada, for example, Paramount had been barred from covering general war activities. The news agencies have been 'so restricted and beaten down by the Allies that they have adopted a defeatist point of view. They will not spend any money covering the war. They will not send men. They will not even get aroused to doing a good job'. To improve the British propaganda methods he recommends that newsreel activities should be encouraged in every part of the Empire, especially Canada. Film thus shot should be 'rushed to London for censorship and later world-wide distribution'. Outlines German newsreel policy to show the kind of competition that England is facing. Factual news pictures of the situation in Europe are 'of vital importance in guiding the Washington Legislators in whatever decision they finally make'. Speed in getting the right sort of material to the United States is essential. 'One other angle that England might work on to its advantage is a check-up system of what pictures are being run around the world and what the audience reaction is to them'. Such a check-up in the U.S. now would show that 'the American newsreels are so hard pressed to keep the balance even that they are taking German propaganda pictures and in some instances putting very nearly pro-Allied commentary upon them'. The writer concludes: 'The above suggestions are not my own but embody the feelings of the American newsreel industry and are really reflections of complaints already printed in the various trade journals'. (A comparative list of shipments received from England and Germany from 27 August to 29 September is appended. A few newspaper clippings had also been attached.)

156   ANON. 'Newsreel men leave for the Western Front'. *The Cinema*, (11 October 1939), p.3, 22.

The previous day a *Cinema* representative had seen cameramen from four of the five companies leave by train for France, the choice from the fifth company having travelled by air the day before. It had been agreed that the War Office would censor all film, the men returning their results to their respective head offices.

1940

157   ANON. 'House of Lords debate on news reel censorship: Under-Secretary for Colonies says Government opposed to stricter forms of control'. *Daily Film Renter*, (25 January 1940), p.1, 7.

The night before Lord Denman had opened a debate on the motion that, 'In the opinion of this House, careful censorship of news films in war time is necessary'. The debate was a sequel to recent comments on a particular issue of *British Paramount News* containing material relating to the homecoming of Unity Mitford and the resignation of Hore-Belisha. Lord Denman felt that G. T. Cummins, the General Manager of the reel had made an error of judgement in magnifying the return of Miss Mitford into a matter of national importance. He was surprised to find there was no censorship whatever of the newsreels, hence his motion. The Marquis of Dufferin and Ava, Parliamentary Secretary for the Colonies, replying for the Government felt that 'what Lord Denman really had in mind was to urge H.M. Government to tighten up the system of censorship on news reels which was already in force'. In war time newspapers and newsreels were entitled voluntarily to submit material to the censor and when they had his permission they were safe from prosecution. He could not make a difference between the newsreels and the press. Finally, he suggested that the House should not accept what appeared to be a perfectly harmless motion which, in fact, had implications wider than perhaps were intended. Lord Denman withdrew his motion.

158   BELL, Oliver. 'Wartime uses of the film'. *The Journal of the Royal Society of Arts*, (5 April 1940), p.467–81.

On page 469 the author, Director of the British Film Institute, suggests that from the propaganda point of view three distinct audiences are to be reached—the Home Front, the members of the belligerent nations and the inhabitants of the neutral countries. On the Home Front films can be used to inform the public about the course of events, to educate it on Government policy, to provide its members with a means of escape from the cares of the day and, lastly, to maintain their morale in face of adversities. For this the newsreels 'are a most important—and probably the most important—type of film'. They could provide a constant and vivid reminder of the war effort. 'The reels could perhaps be less parochial and give more space to the Empire than they do in fact. Here, the trouble seems to lie in the fact that the source of most of their overseas material is the U.S.A. . . . In very general terms the world's news is filtered through the sieve of the American mind before it goes on its way to the rest of the world, and British material goes through the same process before it arrives there'. By and large, however, the reels are doing their work well in presenting in immediate terms their own war effort to the people of Britain. The cinemagazine also has a place in any scheme for promoting morale and conveying information, as does the trailer. On page 475 the author returns to the newsreels. With regard to 'our Allies' the newsreel item is 'of tremendous importance'. However, owing to 'the insipid material which we allow to be taken' Britain does not figure largely on the Dominion news screens. 'The average Britisher hates showing off and blatancy in any form—even in making headline news for the news reels—is repugnant to him but he must learn to show a more lively imagination if we are to get seen even by our sympathisers, who would sooner see something of us than nothing at all.

If only 10% or one minute of each reel were good pro-British stuff there would be no cause to grumble'. (In the discussion which followed Bell's paper Sir Kenneth Clark, Director of Film Division MOI, stated that the speaker had described exactly the kind of programme and policy that the MOI was trying to carry out but he felt that Mr Bell had given 'a sad picture of the state of the news reel'. He went on: 'I do not think it is quite as bad as that and I honestly think that it is improving. A little more than one minute per reel is devoted to the national interest, and I think that if you follow the news reels you will find that more and more space is devoted to things which make our hearts beat faster and make us believe more ardently in the national cause . . . I can honestly say that the Services are now helping us very much more, and, with their help, I think you will find that a great many more things of national interest will be put on to the news reels' . . .)

159   ANON. 'Public and the war newsreels'. *The Cinema*, (12 June 1940), p.25.

Since the possibility of parachutists and fifth columnists becoming active in the U.K. was realised by the public there has been a growing controversy on Tyneside as to whether news films depicting German brutality should be shown. R. Storey, Manager of the News Theatre, Newcastle said: 'The greater part of the newsreels we get deal with the war. Personally, I think the Government want people to realise what modern war is like. I know there is a section of the people who do not like grim newsreels, but it is a fact that we are doing just as well as before the war, if not better'. E. J. Hinge stated he had received letters from both sides, and the bulk were in favour of the present type of newsreel. 'Those in favour', he commented, 'have adopted that attitude, not because they like to see gruesomeness, but because these films reveal the truth about German militarism'.

160   GRIERSON, John. [Comment on reception of British newsreels in U.S.A.] (10 August 1940), 1p. John Grierson Archive, Document no. G4:20:3.

'Too little and too late is the general comment of the British war film record in North America. This applies particularly to feature films. It applies less to newsreels. It has been generally appreciated that in the last three months the newsreel service from England has "greatly improved", "has improved 200%", "has provided 10 to 15 really good stories". There has been "more material and better material", "greater variety of story angles and more interesting story angles, e.g., the industrial angles of the war, the life of the people and avoidance of repetitive troop marching". The origin of these comments is America and may be taken as authoritative'.

161   ANON. 'News Reel: comments of the quarter by *Sight & Sound* contributors'. *Sight & Sound*, vol. 9, no. 35 (Autumn 1940), p.38–40.

The column includes items on a variety of topics of general cinematic interest. A paragraph beginning on page 38 highlights a rumour about Ministry of Information objections to implementing the recommendation of the House of Commons Select Committee on National Expenditure that *British News* should be substituted for the MOI's newsreel service. Gives a brief history of the development of *British News*.

162   HARRISSON, Tom. 'Social Research and the film'. *Documentary News Letter*, vol. 1, no. 11 (November 1940), p.10–12.

Reports on some of the Mass Observation's audience research. Concludes with regard to the newsreels, that there has been a pretty steady decline in their prestige, 'never high', in the past year. The researchers found repeated cases where the newsreels had alienated people by their political bias, by their treatment of emotional topics, by the commentaries (which are often unsympathetic to ordinary people), and had shown by numerous indications that they are sometimes out of touch with the feeling of the moment and even, sometimes, with the permanent feelings of housewives or labourers. The prestige of newsreels seems to have fallen more sharply among middle-class people and among men.

1941

163   *The Film Index. vol. 1: The film as art*, compiled by Workers of the Writers' Program of the Work Projects Administration in the City of New York. New York: Museum of Modern Art Film Library and H. W. Wilson, 1941. xxxvi, 723p.

'Newsreel and Record Films' p.595–610 is an extensive annotated bibliography of American-British items also indicating reviews of early topical films.

164   SANGER, Gerald F. 'A news reel man's conscience'. *Sight & Sound*, vol. 10, no. 38 (Summer 1941), p.22–3.

The *British Movietone News* Editor refutes arguments that 'the only effective film propaganda being done by the Government is the news reels', under such headings as 'Constraints of Security', 'Independent Endorsement' and 'Faking and Reconstruction'. Summarises: 1. 'The news reel, despite censorship, is still an independent purveyor of news and not an official propagandist; 2. as such, its contribution to the maintenance of public confidence is much more effective than if it were known to be Government controlled; 3. the news reels believe that misrepresentation defeats its own object, even if it be labelled "propaganda".'

1942

165   ANSTEY, Edgar. 'The Newsreels . . . (a review)'. *The Spectator*, (9 January 1942), p.35.

As 1941 had closed and 1942 had opened with 'two of the war's best newsreels' Anstey concludes that 'it is possible that the newsreels may yet succeed in adding their due quota to the enormous propaganda power of the film of fact'. There is evidence in *British Paramount News*' annual review that at least one company has imagination and a sense of political realities: 'it is most invigorating to find a newsreel whose approach to the great events of the day is neither infantile nor reactionary'. The second item, the Commando raid on Vaagso was photographed for the War Office partly by Army Film Unit personnel and partly by a newsreel cameraman.

166   COHN, Herbert. 'Running a specialist theatre'. *Sight & Sound*, vol. 11, no. 41 (Summer 1942), p.9–11.

The author, Manager of The Tatler at Chester, had been asked to write an article on managing a specialised theatre during the war. He is 'very strongly of the opinion' that there has been a continual falling off in the interest shown by audiences in the newsreels during the past year, the reason being the great similarity between them all. People are a little tired of seeing tanks and aeroplanes without apparent end: there is, 'at the present time' a surfeit of war items. Political speeches, where the speaker is obviously reading the speech are not well received.

167   *The Manchester Guardian.* Leading article. 'News on the screen'. (30 October 1942), p.4.

'It is reported in the film trade press that the dispute among the five newsreel companies over the operation of the pooling system has been "amicably settled". Under that system "facility visits" are covered in accordance with a rota, and the results are made available to all. That is consistent with current practice in the newspaper world when only a limited number of reporters can be accommodated. But the news-reel system, as at present organised, also requires each company to pool films taken on its own initiative by cameramen working independently in various parts of the world. One company wished to contract out of this part of the agreement; the other four insisted that it be enforced. The Minister of Information, regarding himself as a disinterested referee, threatened to deprive the rebel company of all facilities and of access to the material contributed to the pool by Service film units. It was, of course, obliged to give in. Thus the incident is closed, but the question of public policy remains open. The rebel company, which in peace-time distinguished itself by skilful reporting of the background stories behind the current pictorial news and by forthright editorial comment, regards the news reel as a legitimate branch of the Fourth Estate. Its rivals, themselves content to be sub-editors of official visual handouts and purveyors of a uniform commodity, have forced it to conform. And the Minister of Information, as their agent, cannot wash his hands of responsibility to the film-going public for the consequences'. [The editorial is quoted in full.]

1943

168   McINTYRE, Ronald. *Films without make-up*. Cairo: R. Schindler. 1943. xiv, 340p.

In a long introduction the author, a New Zealand cinematographer, points out that the purpose of the Film Production Units of the Australian, New Zealand, South African, Indian and British armies in the Middle East war theatre during World War 2 was primarily to produce material for their respective countries. It soon became recognised that a pooling system would be advantageous to all and the Ministry of Information in Cairo set up a Film and Photographic Planning Board with the above-mentioned countries represented on it. This body forwarded stories considered to have a wide interest value to England and the U.S.A. where they were incorporated into newsreels and distributed by the largest circuits. The Films Division of the Ministry in Cairo produced and released the newsreel *War Pictorial* which covered the North African campaigns and was released in many languages. F. G. H. 'Gerrie' Taylor, formerly of Gaumont-British and Charles Martin, formerly of Pathé were among those engaged in its production. The introduction of newsfilm in colour is noted—June 1942 'had seen the first battle pictures of World War II filmed in natural colour'—and the activities of the news cameramen are briefly discussed. In the main part of the book the author relates his experiences in obtaining film footage of the war in the Middle East.

169   SINKINS, Melchior A. A. 'A salute to the newsreel cameramen'. *Kinematograph Weekly*, (14 January 1943), p.41–45.

Begins: 'They belong to that fine band of people of the Fourth Service—propaganda and truthful news. With their lives, and by many acts of personal gallantry, and with their craftsmanship they have served the kinemas of this country and those of the United Nations. They have helped to maintain national morale by recording for all time British feats of arms in the battle for freedom and civilization'. Goes on to give 'potted records' and photographs of the British newsreel cameramen covering the Second World War. There is a note by H. W. Bishop, Production Manager of *Gaumont-British News*, on censorship in wartime.

170   ANON. 'Newsreels to be interchangeable: cross-overs working by start of May'. *The Cinema*, (31 March 1943), p.3.

Newsreels have already been reduced in length to 700 feet (instead of 850 feet), the first shortened copies having been published on the Monday of the previous week. District Managers are now working out the details of the change-overs with local exhibitors. It is being arranged that, where necessary, the newsreels will be interchangeable. This will further facilitate the cross-over scheme. Stock allocations for each newsreel have yet to be worked out.

171   ANON. 'A.C.T. seek standard pact with newsreels'. *The Cinema*, (7 April 1943), p.3, 24.

One of the matters recorded in the 10th annual report of the Association of Cine Technicians issued on 6th April was the reforming of the newsreel section. It had been decided that a drive would be made to obtain protection for newsreel members similar to that afforded to other members of the union. It had been decided to approach the Newsreel Association to negotiate a standard agreement. A sub-committee had been appointed to prepare a draft.

172   ANON. 'Concurrent newsreel runs: how the scheme will work'. *Kinematograph Weekly*, (8 April 1943), p.5.

Brief item. Lists six points on newsreel concurrencies, operational generally from May 1st, which were set out in a letter to C.E.A. members issued by W. A. Fuller the previous weekend.

173   ANON. 'British aid newsreel coverage of AEF: better liaison arranged with Army to improve quality of pictures'. *Motion Picture Herald*, vol. 151, no. 2 (10 April 1943), p.16.

The American journal reports that improved liaison between British and American newsreel companies and the United States Army in the European theatre of action was announced that week in London. 'Cameramen for both American and British newsreel companies have been promised fuller access to combat and operation areas, and quicker clearance by headquarters of their film . . . A combined unit of five British cameramen representing the five principal newsreels will be permitted to photograph the war with American forces, from front line positions. It will permit more extensive coverage of action for British screens as well as providing more action material for the United States . . . The new British unit already has been in action . . . The cameramen who filmed the first air actions from U.S. planes were trained by the Army for high altitude operations at a special school established for correspondents . . . Previously newspaper and radio reporters had gone on operational flights but these were said to be the first newsreel cameras permitted aloft . . . '

174   ANON. 'B. of T. confirms Trade's newsreel policy: only one film on first release'. *Kinematograph Weekly*, (15 April 1943), p.11.

Brief item. In answer to a question in the House of Commons to the President of the Board of Trade, Captain Waterhouse said that the shortage of kinematograph film had made it necessary to limit the amount which any one distributor might obtain . . . 'it was possible that theatres would in future be limited by their suppliers to one newsreel on first release . . . '

175   LESTER, Joan. 'Coloured news'. *Reynolds News*. (3 Oct 1943), p.7.

The paper's film critic begins her column: 'One section of film fare is rarely mentioned in columns such as this. That is the current news reels, which are rarely shown to critics. Believing that they are not only significant but the highlight of the programme for many cinema-goers, I think this is a matter for regret. This week I made it my business to see a current news reel and had a surprise. As a journalist, I believe that news is news and a matter for straight, fair and accurate reporting. The news bulletin seems to me to bear a close relationship to a news story. The place for political comment and deduction is in leaders or feature articles. Perhaps "*March of Time*" may be considered the nearest screen parallel to a feature article. But the commentary to this news reel was far from being just straight reporting. It had a very definite political line of its own. Here were remarkable and most intresting pictures of the work of Allied bombers. With them was a commentary to tell us that this was the second front in Europe, that is was not only crippling enemy war industry, but holding down Nazi forces in Europe. The rest of the commentary was on similar lines—hardly unbiased reporting, I think you will agree. War pictures now pass through the Ministry of Information to be shared by the various News Reel agencies, which provide their own commentary based on an M.O.I. handout. I think this is a matter for official attention . . . '

1944

176   ANON. 'M. of I. Challenge to Silverstone'. *Kinematograph Weekly*, (1 June 1944), p.11.

Reports the Ministry of Information statement criticising the suggestion made by Murray Silverstone, Vice-President of 20th-Fox in charge of foreign distribution that there should be a United Nations newsreel. The MOI says the statement comes 'a little late in the day' in view of the fact that the MOI in conjunction with the U.S. Office of War Information and the French National Committee has been producing just such a United newsreel under the title, *Le Monde Libre*, for more than a year, for exhibiting in every kinema in North Africa. The MOI and OWI also jointly produce the Italian newsreel *Notizie del Mondo Libero*. The reels contain material shot by American and British Service Film Units and by civilian cameramen of both countries. An official United Nations newsreel for all European territories after their liberation is also in preparation, to be produced by 'members already chosen' of the Newsreel Association of Great Britain. It is regretted that Mr Silverstone's company refused to co-operate in the pooling of material for this newsreel as this may limit the amount of American material the peoples of liberated Europe will see.

177   ANON. 'United Nations newsreel: Silverstone replies to M. of I.' *Kinematograph Weekly*, (1 June 1944), p.3, 16.

Reports a reply cabled by Murray Silverstone to the MOI's statement that British Movietone had declined to co-operate in the project for a United Newsreel. Mr Silverstone stresses that on May 1st the United Newsreel Corporation of America had unanimously adopted a resolution to make available all its newsreel material for inclusion in the newsreels to be produced under the auspices of the OWI and MOI, and any government in exile in London. The same resolution gives the authorities right to distribute such combined newsreels until such time as normal commercial business is resumed in any liberated area. At present, in certain Allied and neutral territories, two newsreels are being distributed: the United Newsreel, produced by the five newsreel companies of America (which before issue is approved by the OWI) and the British Newsreel made under the auspices of the MOI. As a natural outcome of the resolution adopted Mr Silverstone had visualised the immediate production of a combined newsreel which might be entitled the United *Nations* Newsreel, which should be distributed in those particular territories now served by the United Newsreel and by the MOI reel separately and independently of each other. When the MOI made its statement it must have been completely unaware of the United Newsreel Corporation resolution of some three and a half weeks earlier.

178   ANON. 'Newsreels to be longer: more footage allocated'. *Kinematograph Weekly*, (8 June 1944), p.3.

Briefly notes that discussions between the Board of Trade and the MOI have resulted in additional film stock being made available for newsreels to enable issues of 1,000 feet per week to be made to cover important topical events. The extra footage required will be in the region of one million feet.

179   ANON. 'Free-World newsreels ready'. *Kinematograph Weekly*, (8 June 1944), p.5.

Briefly notes that '*Free World*' newsreels which the MOI, in conjunction with the U.S. OWI, is producing will be ready to be shown in French kinemas the moment the enemy is driven out and civil life resumes something of its pre-war normality. United newsreels are already being shown in Italy. A feature of these newsreels which will eventually be shown everywhere is that the term 'free world' will appear in all titles and a common signature tune will announce it.

180   ANON. 'British newsreels sign basic labor agreement: comprehensive charter is seen as setting pattern for future negotiations'. *Motion Picture Herald*, vol. 156, no. 10 (2 September 1944), p.30.

The American journal reports the joint statement of the Association of Cine Technicians and the Newsreel Association of Great Britain outlining an agreement of terms of employment. The agreement regulates minimum salaries and overtime payment, and provides insurance for employees working outside the company's premises, holidays with pay, and payment for sick leave. It also limits the number of learners who may be employed. The agreement 'obtained in the face of obstinate resistance by certain elements of the Newsreel Association's membership' is seen as a victory for the ACT and a personal triumph for its general secretary, George H. Elvin. 'So pronounced was that opposition, so reluctant the elements mentioned to concede the technicians' demands, that Mr. Elvin was constrained to invoke the interference of the Ministry of Labor'. Full details of the agreement are given.

181   ANON. 'The newsreel "monopoly" attacked: Films Council omission'. *Kinematograph Weekly*, (14 September 1944), p.5.

Attention is called by C. W. Fennell of the Tatler news theatres of Manchester, Leeds and Chester, to the omission from the Film Monopoly Report (Chairman: Albert Palache, HMSO, 1944) to any reference to the alleged newsreel monopoly, owing to the seemingly complete co-ordination between the managements of the five newsreels through their association, which rules prices (doubling them in some cases), enforces common contracts and gives or withholds news service to enforce contracts.

182   SANGER, Gerald L. Letters to the Editor. *The Times* (19 September 1944), p.5.

Replies to an earlier letter complaining about the depiction of death on the screen. There are two schools of thought, the escapist school to which the correspondent belongs and those who demand realism from the newsreel. During wartime the newsreel companies are particularly responsible for presenting an authentic picture of war. Visualization on the screen fills in the details already sketched by newspaper and radio. The newsreel is a member of a trinity conveying information important to public knowledge and national purpose. There have been times when the united influence of all three—Press, radio and film—has been necessary to correct misapprehension and complacency. Victories cannot be won without loss and sacrifice. 'Very rarely, it may even be necessary to shock the public'. The licence to embrace the whole of war's activities is used sparingly and with judgement by the editors of newsreels. *Kinematograph Weekly*, vol. 331, no. 1953 (21 September 1944), p.3, 19, quotes the letter in full under the heading 'Realism in war newsreels: Sanger opposes suppression'.

1945

183   BUCHANAN, Andrew. *Film and the future*. London: Allen and Unwin, 1945. viii, 104p.

Chapter 4, 'Propaganda and the news reel', p.35–47, looks at the newsreel in the light of the experience of World War 2. Looks first at the effect of the MOI on the documentary film then turns to the newsreel, 'the film medium which stood to benefit most during war conditions'. Has it made the best of its opportunity? What is wrong with the basic newsreel apart from too hasty construction? 'It is said to be carelessly constructed, superficial, too brief, and lacking impartiality; in other words, technically, artistically, and politically it fails. If that be so, reasons must be given, for the charge is a serious one'. There are several reasons why sequences in the average newsreel story often lack finish—the first and most important is time: newsreel production can never be slow; then there is the question of commercial control—the first consideration of the newsreel makers is to cater for the regular remunerative market they have established. However, 'the fundamental fact remains that film-makers and their public have been so busy either preparing "news" or imbibing it, that they have not had time to pause to consider what really constitutes news ... A great deal appearing under the title is certainly not news at all, and similarly, a considerable quantity of real news is either withheld, misrepresented or given false emphasis'. 'Long before 1939, partaking of partiality, the news reel and the news bulletin apparently had no alternative but to ally themselves to politics, a move involving an even greater projection of propaganda'. Goes on to give examples of how 'film sequences can be given an entirely new interpretation through the character of the superimposed commentary' and pays tribute to the newsreel crews. Introduces a note of pessimism: 'I have a feeling that the old order of commercial domination and daily output will survive (after the War), will form formidable roadblocks to progress, and will have to be stormed and surmounted' but concludes: 'The day must come when the peoples have at their disposal honest unmanipulated newsreels that truly represent them to each other—allies and enemies alike'.

184   WATTS, Fred. 'Newsreels want end of official control'. *The Cinema*, (3 January 1945), p.54, 59.

The author, Production Manager of *Pathé Gazette*, foresees that the question of controls will be one of the problems that the newsreels will have to face in the postwar period. With the ending of war there can be little or no justification for many of the restrictions on the gathering of news, and filming of countless events and ceremonies. He is looking forward to 'the old opportunities of free competition, and an increase in the film-stock supply to help (the newsreel companies) to satisfy the public's great thirst for news in films', and to the return of the technicians who are now serving with the armed forces. With the increase in air lines and rapid locomotion in general after the War the world will be a smaller place. Continents far away will be just around the corner. Scoops and specials will be sent by air and television with its news possibilities is nearer than the film trade thinks.

185   ANON. 'Camp horrors to be screened: M. of I. and newsreels using Buchenwald film'. *Daily Film Renter*, (26 April 1945), p.3.

Briefly reports that in the House of Commons the day before the Minister of Information was asked if films had been taken showing the conditions at the concentration camp in Buchenwald, and if such films would be shown to the public so that the atrocities which the German people had endorsed might be widely known. Mr Brendan Bracken, had replied: 'Yes sir. There is ample film material showing the conditions at the concentration camp in Germany that is available for incorporation in newsreels. I understand the film companies are making use of it so far as they can. Material is also being used by the M. of I. for making a film for showing in Germany. A version will also be available to audiences here'.

186   ANON. 'Atrocity scenes: C.E.A. advice'. *Kinematograph Weekly*, (3 May 1945), p.3.

Brief item: The C.E.A. advises all members showing the newsreels of German prison camp atrocities to make an announcement immediately prior to the showing of the newsreel to the effect that 'the newsreel about to follow depicts gruesome scenes of German atrocities in prison camps'. Goes on: 'The attention of parents or others with children is directed to that fact and that there is an opportunity for the children to leave the kinema' . . . 'Where the Universal newsreel is shown the announcement is unnecessary, as it forms an introduction to the reel itself'.

187   ANON. 'Election newsreels were a mistake: sharp C.E.A. protest'. *Daily Film Renter*, (12 July 1945), p.3.

Briefly reports the previous day's adoption by the C.E.A. General Council of a report on newsreels and the Election from its Legal, Finance and Parliamentary Committee. The Committee was satisfied that the adoption by the newsreel companies of the same system as the BBC in connection with General Elections in an attempt to ensure impartiality for all political parties by taking all party politicians in turn was a mistake. In future General Elections the newsreels should only give topical news.

188   FENNELL, Corry W. 'Television will be no rival—what we want is longer newsreels!' *Kinematograph Weekly* (9 August 1945), p.5.

The author, owner of a chain of newsreel theatres in the North of England, believes that after the war the development of the newsreel will be measured not only by the desire of the producers to create better and better reels but also by the wishes of the people. Before the war the newsreels—with notable exceptions—confined themselves to bringing to the screen planned events: 'anything controversial was feared as the plague'. The postwar citizen will want realism. Believes the newsreels should devote about one third of their length to 'world events and living (including sport), which is entirely away from war, war problems, politics and international affairs'. There would be ample film stock to do this 'if redundant and unwelcome propaganda trailers were cut out'. Future newsreels will be interpretative in their treatment of world affairs and this will be in response to public demand, and they will be in colour. Television will work along with, and further increase the importance of newsreels. Newsreels should be restored to their pre-war length at the earliest possible moment.

189   ANON. 'Newsreel politics criticised'. *Kinematograph Weekly*, (20 September 1945), p.13.

Snippet. 'Criticism of the methods of newsreels adopted in connection with the General Election has been conveyed to the Newsreel Association, the C.E.A. General Council was informed. This has been acknowledged, and it has been intimated that all the points raised will be borne in mind for future reference'.

1946

190   ASHWOOD, Terry, 'Newsreels in war-time: the North African campaign'. *The Journal of the British Kinematograph Society*, vol. 9, no. 1 (January-March 1946), p.17–19.

A text delivered to a symposium arranged by the Newsreel Association and read to the British Kinematograph Society on November 14th, 1945. The author, a cameraman with Pathé Pictures, gives an anecdotal account of his experiences in the Western Desert from 1941.

191   BONNETT, Sidney, 'The liberation of Europe'. *The Journal of the British Kinematograph Society*, vol. 9, no. 1 (January-March 1946), p.21–25.

A text delivered to a symposium arranged by the Newsreel Association and read to the British Kinematograph Society on November 14th, 1945. The author, a cameraman with *Gaumont-British News*, gives an anecdotal account of his experiences in France, Belgium and Holland.

192   MURRAY, Leslie. 'The Norwegian campaign'. *The Journal of the British Kinematograph Society*, vol. 9, no. 1 (January-March 1946), p.26–27.

A text delivered to a symposium arranged by the Newsreel Association and read to the British Kinematograph Society on November 14th, 1945. The author, Assistant Editor of *Universal News*, recounts an experience in Norway with cameraman Sidney Bonnett in which the author sustained the serious injuries that ended his career as a wartime cameraman.

193   TOZER, Alec. 'Newsreels in war-time: war filming in the Far East'. *The Journal of the British Kinematograph Society*, vol. 9, no. 1 (January-March 1946), p.19–21.

A text delivered to a symposium arranged by the Newsreel Association and read to the British Kinematograph Society on November 14th, 1945. The author, a cameraman with *British Movietone News*, gives an anecdotal account of his experiences, beginning in Burma at the end of 1941 then on to India and China, returning to Burma again in 1943. Stresses the difficulties of transporting camera equipment.

194   SANGER, Gerald F. 'Propaganda and the News-reel'. *Sight & Sound*, vol. 15, no. 59 (Autumn 1946), p.79–80.

The Editor of *British Movietone News* makes the point that no two political opponents can agree upon the nature of propaganda. Asks: 'would a news-reel not be denying a great many of its legitimate functions if it did not record events which conduce to the upholding of established institutions?' Touches on the pursuit of objectivity. The liberty of the Press should be sustained in its extension to the newsreels and, the film industry should back the Newsreel Association to the hilt in maintaining the principle inviolate. The editors of news-reels, however, should recognise those limitations involved in their medium which do not affect newspapers. There are occasions when an individual charged with a responsibility must flout what he knows will be popular opinion and preach an unwelcome gospel. It is 'a source of constant regret' to the writer that 'we, who had the newsreel pictures of Nazi bellicosity, did not do more in those days to draw public attention to their significance'.

195   ANON. 'Newsreels in demand again by Eire'. *The Cinema*, (16 October 1946), p.3, 40.

Reports moves being made by officials of the Irish Republic to secure renewed distribution of British newsreels. At the outbreak of the war the newsreels had been so heavily censored by the Irish authorities and war scenes banned that little or nothing was left of the original make up. Most of the companies, consequently, ceased distribution. *British Movietone News*, however, subsequently prepared and distributed a special Irish edition but this was withdrawn when further cuts in raw stock supplies were made. No British reels are now distributed in the country and newsreel chiefs are unanimous that renewed distribution depends on an improvement in raw stock supplies. In the meantime, a new Irish company, Eire Films Ltd., has been formed with the purpose of making Irish newsreels and film magazines.

196   ANON. 'No hangings on newsreels'. *Kinematograph Weekly*, (17 October 1946), p.3.

Reports that the Nuremberg hangings would not be shown in the newsreels. In reply to a question in the House of Commons the previous Tuesday by Anthony Eden, the Prime Minister had replied that the Allied Control Commission had decided that no film or photographs should be taken of the executions.

1947

197   *The Factual Film*. 'The news film'. *The Factual Film: the Arts Enquiry: a survey sponsored by the Dartington Hall Trustees*. London, 1947. Chapter 4, p.136–143.

An analysis of the organisation and coverage of the five national British newsreels with a section on the MOI official newsreels and the American *March of Time* series. Discusses the wartime rota system, concluding that 'the rota has tended to kill initiative and a tedious sameness in the issues of all five newsreels has been apparent from the inception of the system; censorship—'under the rota system material released has been automatically censored on security grounds'; and production costs—'£1000 is a tentative estimate of cost for an average week's production of two issues'; and content—'the usual content of the majority of pre-war British newsreels was trivial' and the newsreel companies look forward to a return to the pre-war position now that their wartime role is over: 'the main aim of the newsreel directorate is therefore to be as complaisant as possible, to be inoffensive by rule, and when forced by exceptional circumstances to deal with social and political issues, to play safe'. On page 88 (Chapter 2—'the documentary film during the war') there is a paragraph about the newsreel, *The Free World*.

198   ANON. 'Producers told Newsreels say "no" to training scheme; apprenticeship drive starts this week'. *Kinematograph Weekly*, (12 June 1947), p.8.

Reports that members of the British Film Producers Association were informed the previous week that the Newsreel Association was the only trade association to have dropped out of the production industry's apprenticeship scheme.

199   ANON. 'Three union agreements this week'. *The Daily Film Renter*, (30 July 1947), p.3, 9.

Reports the signing of an agreement covering working conditions and salary rates by the Newsreel Association and the ACT. The agreement, covering about 200 workers, contains 25 clauses and replaces the document of 1944. Minimum rates are set out. Members of the Newsreel Association retain the right to negotiate future individual contracts with employees, but the terms and conditions of all such contracts shall be not less favourable to the employees concerned than are contained in the agreement. Complete details of the agreement are given.

200   SHAW ASHTON, D. 'My prize-winning newsreel'. *Amateur Cine World*, vol. 3, no. 7 (August 1947), p.315–18.

'Newsreel shots should not be left to chance. They should be planned in advance'. The amateur one described earned considerable praise for its construction when it was awarded the *Daily Mail* cup in a contest organised by the Institute of Amateur Cinematographers. This first of two articles describes, with sketches, the preparation of the shooting script.

201   SHAW ASHTON, D. 'Filming a newsreel'. *Amateur Cine World*, vol. 3, no. 8 (September 1947), p.355–58.

'Even the best newsreels rarely attain the same high quality of photography to which one is accustomed in other films. The newsreel cameraman cannot wait for an improvement in the weather but is bound to shoot his subject whatever the prevailing conditions'. In this second of two articles the author describes how the shooting of his amateur prize-winning newsreel worked out in practice.

202   ANON. 'Newsreel agreement signed'. *The Cine-Technician: the Journal of the Association of Cine-Technicians*, vol. 13, no. 68 (September-October 1947).

Gives full details of the new agreement. ACT newsreel members have gained increased salaries and improved working conditions. While the advances are not so spectacular as those for feature technicians, neither were the Union's original demands. There is satisfaction that no breakdown in negotiations between the two parties occurred, as had happened in 1944 when an independent arbitrator had to be called in.

1948

203   MORGAN, Guy. *Red roses every night: an account of London cinemas under fire*. London: Quality Press, 1948. 127p. + 16p. of plates.

P.69–71 have some comments on audience reactions to the newsreels, e.g.: 'The enjoyment or non-enjoyment of programmes was always profoundly affected by the newsreels. Dunkirk, Singapore, or any of the other major tragedies of the war upset the balance of people's minds. The newsreel, while it was still hot and fresh was terrifically real; although paradoxically, the documentary which is simply news in retrospect, was never really popular'. '1944 was a pretty satisfactory year for the cinema. The news was good . . . We cheered the newsreels almost as if we dared to let our feelings have vent for the first time'.

204   CAVE, G. Clement. 'Newsreels must find a new policy'. *Penguin Film Review*, no. 7 (1948), p.50–4.

The author who is Editor of *Pathé News* takes as his starting point the following assertion from the chapter on news film in *The Factual Film*: 'The main aim of the newsreel directorate is therefore to be as complaisant as possible, to be inoffensive by rule, and when forced by exceptional circumstances to deal with social and political issues, to play safe'. Accuses the newsreel editors and exhibitors of having played safe for too long: they have far too comfortable an assumption about public taste and have failed to recognise that the war brought about a great change in public outlook and taste. The newsreels still hesitate to take a chance. Claims that *Pathé News* is the only one attempting to face social and economic issues. The author has developed the technique which gives his product a *March of Time* treatment: there is one main title and one story which form the theme and shape of the reel. 'Into that setting is packed the world news, supported by a commentary which reviews, explains, comments and is all of a piece. It is an editorial must that the commentary is positive'. In future there can be little room in the newsreels for 'the nonsense of a Texas rodeo or a Miami beach parade': a new set of values must take over. 'There will be room for television and a bright future for the news film only if newsreels become invigorated'.

1949

205   BRITISH BROADCASTING CORPORATION. *BBC Year Book 1949*. London: BBC, 1949. 152p.

The section 'Television', p.93–95 notes: 'In January [1948] the first BBC *Newsreel* was televised; a weekly edition was soon extended to two editions a week'.

206   DORTÉ, P. H. 'The B.B.C. Television newsreel'. *BBC Quarterly*, vol. 3, no. 4 (January 1949), p.229–34.

The author, Head of Television Outside Broadcasts and Films at the BBC, discusses the history and production of the BBC newsreel. Early experience provided the formula for the compilation of a regular television newsreel—a news film containing more than one story: a total running time of about fifteen minutes and with not less than two or more than seven minutes devoted to one item. The $8\frac{1}{2}$ minute commercial newsreel rarely devotes more than two minutes in all to one subject. Raises the question of how long a filmed news-event remains 'news'. Foresees each major national television system (in different countries) having an eventual daily international television newsreel, shot, in the main, by television film-cameramen and edited and commented on specifically for the home television audiences.

207   ANON. 'Official attitude of the Association of Cine Technicians'. *Impact*, (Spring 1949), p.26–7.

Expresses grave concern over the expansion of rota-covered stories by the member companies of the Newsreel Association. The Newsreel Section of the ACT does not regard these inter-newsreel arrangements as anything but a direct attack on the full employment of its members, e.g. *British Paramount News* has reduced its actual production staff to less than a score and is operating with only four cameramen on the road; several cases have occurred where cameramen, on independent assignment by their employer company, in applying for on-the-spot facilities from the government department concerned, have been told by officials that the 'material is to be rota'. The quality of rota material shows a marked lack of the sense of responsibility due the job. Each firm has received over 100,000 feet of rota cover in the last nine months: the average amount of material used is surmised to vary from eight to fifteen per cent: many of the dupes supplied are a disgrace to the trade because of hurried processing. However, 'already shorn of much independence by ministerial influence the newsreels are being pushed into second place by their coming competitor, television'.

208   TUNWELL, Alf. 'Newsreel monopoly: (a) personal statement'. *Impact* (Spring 1949), p.24–6.

The author, Chief Cameraman of Telenews, accuses the Newsreel Association of prolonging the rota system (including the royal rota) that was introduced during the War because the system, which was 'a wise and convenient arrangement' for wartime, was just 'too convenient'. The Association had discovered that speaking on behalf of 'all' newsreels it had more power to deal with government departments and public relations officers. The system also saves costs. Accuses the Association of monopolising the most important news events, e.g. for six months in 1946 the Association had prevented *Metro News* (formed by Metro-Goldwyn Mayer) from including pictures of the Royal Family, as well as news of other British institutions and important occasions. The newsreel companies refused to supply BBC Television with newsreels (as they had done before the War) which resulted in the formation of the BBC Television Newsreel Unit. The Association is currently trying to keep out an all-British newsreel unit established in Britain by Telenews, a new American company. Advises the Association to consider whether their monopoly is really in the nation's interest, 'for when the television deluge hits this country, as it will, newsreels as we know them today will be no match for the news service that television will pipe daily into our homes'.

209   SHERIDAN, Paul. 'British Movietone choose'. *Impact*, (Summer 1949), p.15.

Accuses *British Movietone News*, with a specific example, of 'making' the news, with regard to the dock strike. 'Evidence is mounting that the whole structure of the newsreels is built on deliberately biased reporting', favouring the Tory Party. The newsreel companies are making political films that are 'boringly partisan, stupidly discriminating and . . . reactionary'. The American-owned Telenews unit is showing the Newsreel Association how the job should be done with bright newsworthy features that do not make a travesty of the news.

210   ANON. 'Free comment'. *Sequence: film quarterly*, no. 8 (Summer 1949), p.47–8.

The second half of this editorial is devoted to a critique of the newsreels. It accuses newsreel producers of imposing 'a standard equivalent to that of the worst penny papers, more dangerous because the means at their disposal are even more potent'. Refers to the article on the newsreel monopoly by Sheridan in *Impact*. Goes on: the best things in newsreels are usually the sports items, 'vividly shot and well edited'. 'The rest is a disorderly, Big Five mélange based mainly on sensationalism, drenched in vulgar music, slapped together with a loud, unctuous commentator, without regard for chronology, place or relative importance'. Civil wars are made to look alike 'by pontifical clichés about refugees, bandits, "widespread chaos and suffering" and "a future in the balance".' With regard to political bias, the newsreels are 'firmly anti-Communist—which is not to condemn them—but what is disgusting is their readiness to turn any incident into a vehicle for exploiting this, for repeating empty, irrelevant, jingoistic slogans. Offers, as an example, a recent story on the civil war in China by *British Movietone News* in which the commentator informed the viewer over shots of refugees, how thousands were fleeing the Red terror and referred to the tragedy of the 'Amethyst', reinforcing this with library shots of the American 'Panay' being shelled ten years earlier. 'The implication of a political connection between the two events is as unmistakeable as it is unfounded'. 'Political fairness, from the General Election onwards has never been a hall-mark of newsreels'. Any opposition to newsreels from the outside has to break down not only a monopoly of inbred popular taste, but of coverage and distribution. 'If the COI were to produce a newsreel it would be welcome for its discrimination and decency, its respect for human dignities, even at the cost of dullness, and because it would also be able to overrule the Newsreel Association and all its works . . .'

211 ANSTEY, Edgar. 'The magazine film'. *The Penguin Film Review*, no. 9 (May 1949), p.17–21.

Anticipates the Central Office of Information's forthcoming screen magazine *This Modern Age*. The author, as a contributor to this magazine, and to the *March of Time*, identifies both as 'films of purpose'—they have something to say of more consequence than the manner of the saying. Quotes the favourite exhortation of Louis de Rochemont—'Never call your shot', meaning never use commentary for what is sufficiently obvious to the eye. Looks at examples of other series, e.g. the American *Inside Nazi Germany* and the Canadian *World in Action*. Though coherence and vitality of exposition are more to the point of the magazine film than beautiful photography, ideally one employs both. Advises the editors of *This Modern Age* to devote some study to the precision of the ideological and emotional relationship between word and image achieved in the early *March of Time* items. In some examples of *This Modern Age* that the writer has so far seen the editing has been loose and undynamic and the consistently beautiful photography has resulted in a kind of travelogue of ideas rather than an integrated conception of the theme. The new magazine is nonetheless finding a higher degree of precision in its commentaries than the genre has yet experienced and is less stereotyped in its camerawork than the older magazines.

212 ANON. 'Bernstein flays the newsreels'. *The Daily Film Renter*, (6 July 1949), p.3, 10.

Reports Granada's decision to cancel newsreels, at their theatres. Mr Sidney L. Bernstein says the decision was taken because in Granada's opinion the newsreels, with one exception, 'are of poor quality, lacking the sense of journalistic selectivity and showmanship' and they invariably bored their audiences. In the Bernstein questionnaire of 1946–47 only 41% of patrons thought the newsreels good. Since then, the newsreels have further deteriorated. The newsreels 'show incompetence in production; often political bias, and many items are socially outmoded'. They often publicise feature films controlled by their parent companies, which are booked to Granada's opposition kinemas, and sometimes go so far as to publicise society and political friends. Granada's public are interested in screen news and if good newsreels are available the company will show them, providing the newsreel companies have sufficient confidence in their films to take the normal hazards of business and allow exhibitors to cancel contracts if patrons are not satisfied. The company excepted from Granada's strictures is *Pathé News* which 'has displayed showmanship and resourcefulness'. The film trade should watch the BBC television newsreel which 'is rightly gaining an increasing number of regular viewers and admirers'. The alleged raw stock shortage does not affect the issue.

213 HARDY, Douglas. 'The technician replies'. *Film Industry*, vol. 7, no. 52 (14 July 1949), p.4, 5, 16.

'The news that the Granada group of 55 cinemas is to end its newsreel contracts is the latest blow against the oldest branch of the industry'. Since the war, successive economy waves have hit the newsreels. First came the cuts by American companies following the 75% tax—these have never been restored though staffs were cut to the minimum level and below. And there was the Universal-Gaumont merger. The effect of all these has been to reduce coverage. In the main, the reels are now concerned with London and foreign news because such coverage is relatively cheap. The stringent economy measures have also meant the continuation, in one form or another, of the wartime rota. 'All newsreels are the same these days'. Looming up is the threat of television, 'more potential than real at present'. Agrees with Sidney Bernstein that the newsreels lack a 'broad vision'. The 'hardy annual' assignments give the cameraman little scope for creativity. The public is now interested in 'a journalistic approach to the problems of the hour', an approach which has been proved successful 'in recent years'. To counter television the newsreels should forget 'the hot news' and become commentators on current events, striving 'to present a fair picture of both sides'. Suggests the production of one longer reel per week, instead of the bi-weekly shorter ones. A revival of public interest can only come from a new and forceful outlook.

214   THOMAS, Howard. 'The newsreel's future'. *Film Industry*, vol. 7, no. 52 (14 July 1949), p.5, 16.

In an interview with Pat Bowman, Thomas, the chairman of the Newsreel Association and producer-in-chief of Associated British-Pathé—the one reel excepted from Sidney Bernstein's criticism—discusses his approach to current problems of newsreel technique and considers the ways in which 'the topical film' may develop in the future. The basic trouble is that the reels are all suffering by comparison with wartime coverage. Newsreels could do with less sport and society weddings and similar occasions have had their day. He discusses Pathé's quarterly two-reeler *Summing Up* in which world events are put in perspective at the end of each quarter. The Pathé bi-weekly reel now often contains records of events that have not just been strung together side by side but have deliberately been juxtaposed for significance and emphasis. On a few occasions a whole reel has been devoted to one theme. A newsreel cameraman needs a news sense but 'nowadays a lot more thought goes into the preliminary preparation of an ordinary newsreel'. BBC television is not competing to any great extent with the newsreels at the the moment but it is able to and probably will take on more current events and live sport. For spectacular events the reels have the advantage of the large screen. There is no evidence that audiences are not responding favourably to newsreels. However, the newsreel, like the newspaper must change with the public, or preferably, be one step ahead of it. Audience research can help.

215   *Tribune*. 'Beware of the newsreels'. *Tribune*, no. 656 (5 August 1949), p.1–2.

The article is written by a film technician but it also represents the editorial view of *Tribune*. Accuses the film trade of being conscious or semi-conscious parties to a conspiracy to get rid of the Labour Government. In the past it was confined to veiled innuendoes, pointed omissions and a glamourisation of Churchill and prominent Tories, but now the newsreels have got down to their business in earnest and are making plans for the general election. Newsreel coverage of the Labour Party Conference in Blackpool was distorted by the judicious use of camera angle and editing. The newsreels also concoct news. At a time when the newsreel companies are supposed to be suffering from a shortage of film stock they have accumulated over a long period a tremendous library of anti-Government shots ready for the general election. In addition, they have just completed a film on behalf of the Tory Central Office. 'The general election newsreels are to provide the final bombshell'. The public should be informed of the cinematic tricks of the newsreels.

216   ANON. 'Craig replies to newsreel "bias" charge'. *The Cinema*, (10 August 1949), p.3, 10.

In a reply to the charges of newsreel political bias made in the *Tribune* leading article, Sir Gordon Craig speaking for *British Movietone News* is quoted as saying: 'Never have newsreel cameramen been sent out with instructions to shoot unfavourable angles whether the story be political or otherwise. British newsreels are edited entirely without any regard for party policy. The newsreels have no "plans" for the forthcoming General Election and, the very fact that the Labour Party is in power has meant that in the news of the past few years they have received the major share of the footage'. He went on to deny emphatically any suggestion that the newsreel which he controlled was working for the Conservative Central Office: 'Our Shorts Department have been commissioned by the Conservative Party to make an instructional film for their agents. This department is entirely separate from the newsreel organisation . . .'

217   ANON. 'Up and down the street by Onlooker'. *The Cinema*, (10 August 1949), p.6.

The column contains two items on newsreels. The first compliments *British Movietone News* on the exclusive pictures from Hong Kong on the arrival of the 'Amethyst' there which Sir Gordon Craig had just previewed for the columnist. 'The newsreels, in the "Amethyst" exploit, have had an opportunity to demonstrate their enterprise, and Movietone have taken full advantage of it'. The second item takes issue with the *Tribune* article. 'It's nonsense to suggest . . . that the newsreels have a "plan" to throw out the Socialist Government'. The newsreel companies' 4,000 customers have made it abundantly clear to the companies that they will not stand for any political platforms whatsoever. Over the previous 18 months they had made 'one or two complaints' about bias in COI films. These complaints were discussed with Herbert Morrison who, although he maintained the items concerned did not contain propaganda, also made it clear he would see that the COI films never would. Finally, 'to suggest that Movietone is politically interested because of Lord Rothermere's connection is such a distortion as to make one gasp'.

218   SANGER, Gerald F. 'Beware of the newsreels: [a reply]'. Letters to the Editor. *Tribune*, (12 August 1949), p.14.

Takes issue with the previous week's article. Categorically states 1) that the newsreels have not yet made any 'plans' for the General Election, 2) that the American interests in British newsreels have never sought to influence the British people politically, 3) that British newsreels are edited free of party political prejudice, 4) that the Labour Party, by the very fact of being in power, have received the *lion's share* of space in British newsreels during the (previous) twelve months and over the whole period since the General Election of 1945, and 5) that newsreel cameramen have never been sent out with instructions to shoot unfavourable angles on any personality whatever, political or otherwise. Goes on to discuss specific *British Movietone News* stories and the film made at Brighton Studios for the Tory Central Office —'the real character (of the latter) may now be revealed as an instructional film commissioned by the Conservative Central Office for the instruction of Party Agents and workers'; it was never destined for inclusion in a newsreel. Finally challenges *Tribune* to publish his letter.

219   *Tribune*. 'Beware of the newsreels: [an editorial reply to Gerald F. Sanger's letter]'. *Tribune*, (12 August 1949), p.14.

The editors refer to the 'coziness of the monopoly' which allows Mr Sanger to claim that he is speaking for all British Newsreels. They list the directors of *British Movietone News* and ask, whether 'these objective gentlemen never allow their political outlooks to influence the product they are putting on the market'. Quotes Sidney L. Bernstein's view that the newsreels 'show incompetence in production, often political bias, and many items are socially outmoded'. Affirms editorial support for the article. Finally takes issue with Sanger about the non-filming of the big miners' galas.

220   WARTER, Sir Philip. '[Beware of the] newsreels: more denials: [a further reply]'. Letters to the Editor. *Tribune*, (19 August 1949), p.14

The author, Chairman of Associated British Cinemas Ltd., states that the article of 5th August is 'an excellent piece of fiction . . . utterly devoid of foundation in fact'. The statement that he and other directors of ABC are conscious or semi-conscious parties to a conspiracy to get rid of the (Labour) Government is 'stupid and malicious'. Mr Bernstein is only refusing to book newsreels for exhibition because 'they have little or no effect on box office takings'. Disagrees that the American film trade is seeking to influence the British people politically.

221   WRIGHT, E. J. H. '[Beware of the] newsreels: more denials: [a further reply]'. Letters to the Editor. *Tribune* (19 August 1949), p.14.

The author, Editor of *British Paramount News*, briefly refutes the 'disgraceful and untrue remarks' made in the article of 5th August. 'It is sufficient to say that (Paramount's) records will prove how wrong is the writer of the article in question'. The context of the article is 'too ridiculous for (him) to digress upon it further'.

222   *Tribune*. '[Beware of the] newsreels: more denials: [a further editorial reply]'. *Tribune*, (19 August 1949), p.14.

Repeats charges of political bias revealed in the newsreels and enlists support of Sidney Bernstein's remarks again. *Tribune* would not be opposed to the expression of different political views on the screen if the cinema industry, and the newsreel companies in particular, 'were not so heavily monopolised and heavily inclined to favour one side'.

223   WYATT, M. A. '[Beware of the] newsreels: an American view': [a further letter on the subject]'. Letters to the Editor. *Tribune*, (26 August 1949), p.14.

The author, an American visitor to Britain, saw four British newsreels and notes that while Mr Churchill was warmly and generously covered, 'practically all' the shots of the Prime Minister's speech to the United Nations' Association 'were from a distance and somewhat to the rear; almost the only close-up was partly devoted, unncessarily, to recording a grimace'. In addition, Mr Attlee's speech was hard to follow, 'as the sound was apparently reduced'. 'After the closing sentences, which were almost inaudible, came the commentator's voice, loud, clear and definitely sarcastic: "These are words to remember!"' The author's impression 'so far' of the British newsreels strongly support *Tribune*'s charges.

224   ROGERSON, J. C. '*Tribune* hits at newsreels'. *The Cine-Technician: the Journal of the Association of Cine-Technicians*, vol. 15, no. 80 (September-October 1949), p.136–38.

Regrets that *Tribune* should have published its attack on the newsreels (August 5th) 'without consulting the appropriate section of A.C.T. in order to establish the facts'. Accuses the writers of not understanding the way newsreels are produced e.g. camera angles are mostly Hobson's choice: as picture and sound track are on a single negative the sound cameraman is responsible for the 'rough cut' of any political speech he covers—it is very easy to run out of film when switching the camera on and off while attempting to record the important sections of the speech: a 'silent' cameraman in the meantime takes a number of audience reaction shots including three 'personalities'; the combined material then goes back to the cutter who may have to cut negatives (for there is rarely time to get a print): in the main politicians have themselves to blame for the coverage they get—neither main party provides adequate facilities for newsreel cameramen. Takes issue with *Tribune*'s charge that newsreel cameramen sometimes 'make' news. Agrees that political bias exists but feels that this complaint is exaggerated. Most technicians would 'go a long way toward agreement' with Sidney Bernstein's remarks. Contrary to the belief of *Tribune*'s editors, who credit the newsreels with Machiavellian policy, the trouble is that the newsreels have no policy at all beyond a negative one, which says—'Don't try anything new'. In future *Tribune* should approach the A.C.T. Executive Council for the right information rather than rush into print on the word of 'film technicians' who would probably lose their jobs if the film monopolists got to know their names.

1950

225   BLAND, W. S. 'The Development of the sound news-reel'. *British Kinematography: the Journal of the British Kinematograph Society*, vol. 17, no. 2 (August 1950), p.50–3.

A paper read to the BKS at a meeting, 'The Evolution of the News-reel', on 5 April 1950. The author, from Associated British Pathé, discusses the transition from silent to sound reels, 'a revolution which came virtually overnight'. The new film speed of 24 frames per second, demanded to extend the range of recorded frequencies, and meant a slowing up of processing and added 50% to the amount of material to be handled. At the outset re-recording was not considered. Silent sub-titles told the essence of a story shot with synchronised sound. It was some time before the art of narration was developed and the commentary was on occasions recorded live on location. With the development of dubbing equipment, libraries of effects and music, the early preoccupation with natural sound waned. Lists the functions of the various ingredients of a newsreel soundtrack: 1) Commentary which serves to amplify the information presented visually or not obviously, and to link scenes; 2) sync. sound which serves to enhance authenticity, restoring the camera's reputation for truth, and to enhance the dramatic value of the action, aided where necessary by 3) library sound effects and 4) music which also raises the dramatic value, and links disconnected visuals. Goes on to discuss early equipment and advances in technique. Ends with a look at the current technical situation and future developments.

226   GORDON, Kenneth. 'The early days of the news-reels'. *British Kinematography: the Journal of the British Kinematograph Society*, vol. 17, no. 2 (August 1950), p.47–50.

A paper read to the BKS at a meeting, 'The Evolution of the News-reel', on 5 April 1950. The author, from Associated British-Pathé, is also Newsreel Vice-President of the Association of Cinematograph & Allied Technicians. Reviews the early history from the filming by Robert W. Paul of the Derby in 1896. First regular news coverage was by the Biograph Company. In 1898, A. J. West inaugurated his combination of news and interest films of the Royal Navy, which for so many years ran in the West End of London under the title *Our Navy*. W. K. L. Dickson and J. Rosenthal photographed the Boer War and the Russo-Japanese War for the Biograph Company. Mentions kinds of cameras used by *Pathé Gazette*, *Gaumont Graphic*, *Warwick Chronicle*, *Topical Budget*, *Williamson News* and *Eclair Journal*. The Provincial Cinematograph Theatres had darkrooms in their chief theatres. Local films were taken, processed in the kinema and shown the same night. Colour was being experimented with. Highlights the arrangements for photographing King Edward's funeral, the Coronation of King George V and the Delhi Durbar. During the First World War the newsreel firms banded together and formed the War Office Films Committee. The Government bought up *Topical Budget* and ran it as an Official War News. In the early Twenties a newsreel war developed, the main cause being the granting of exclusive rights for major sporting events. Activities of the pirates.

The Charles Urban company displays cameras used to cover the Delhi Durbar 1911 (courtesy of the National Film Archive)

227   THOMAS, Howard. 'The future of the news-reel'. *British Kinematography: the Journal of the British Kinematograph Society*, vol. 17, no. 2 (August 1950), p.53–5.

A paper read to the BKS at a meeting, 'The Evolution of the News-reel', on 5 April 1950. The author, from Associated British Pathé, points out that of the five British reels Pathé and Gaumont-British have the largest distribution, reaching more than a thousand kinemas each. All the reels appear twice a week and they are limited in length to a maximum of 700 feet. The newsreels are the only films subject to stock rationing (recently relaxed but not rescinded) because of the huge quantity they use—something like one and a half million feet each week. Because of the supplemental contract, newsreels are tied to the kinemas which booked them during the early part of the war, with prices still at pre-war level. The reels are also limited to fixed release times, on Mondays and Thursdays, falling in with the film industry's general transport service. The competition of television may result in greater efforts for topicality and the future may bring weekend work as a regular practice. In general, television will not harm the cinema. Newsreels, however, are the first branch of the industry to be directly affected by the new medium: it is inevitable that they will lose their former advantage of urgency and topicality. There are already daily TV newsreels in New York. Big shows like Royal Weddings, Grand Nationals, Cup Finals etc. will always stand repetition on the big screen. Two courses are open to the reels; 1) to alter their shape and presentation so there is compensation for the loss of topicality and 2) to get into television themselves, which is outside their control at the moment as the whole question is being considered by the Beveridge Committee and the film industry has applied for the right to televise. In the meantime, newsreels should become more interpretative, *explaining* to the public in an entertaining way the background to the news and its significance.

228   ANON. 'Protest this week on newsreel increases'. *To-day's Cinema*, (18 September 1950), p.3.

Reports briefly an informal meeting of West End newsreel theatre owners on the previous Friday to consider action in protest against the proposed increased charges which the Newsreel Association had said it intended to introduce on October 1st. The owners decided to refrain from independent action pending the outcome of talks between the Cinematograph Exhibitors' Association and the Newsreel Association.

229   ANON. 'Newsreel camera aces'. *The Cinema*, (20 September 1950), p.15.

A page of captioned photographs of six well-known newsreel cameramen, John Turner, who 'specialises in filming Royalty'; Jack Harding who 'always works alone'; "Eddy" Edmonds, 'the most widely experienced man in the newsreel business'; John Cotter who with the Royal Rota cameraman 'obtained the first pictures of Prince Charles with his mother and father'; Peter Cannon who 'covers news events where quality is of supreme importance—he was nearest newsreel man to King George VI during his coronation', and S. R. G. Bonnett, who 'was in the first aircraft to fly over Mount Everest' and who is Gaumont-British's aerial photography expert.

230   ANON. 'N.-Western CEA protest on newsreel costs'. *Kinematograph Weekly*, (21 September 1950), p.12.

Reports a meeting of the North-Western branch of the CEA in Liverpool on the previous Friday. Concern was expressed over the burden that would be laid upon small exhibitors called upon to pay 'double the ordinary fees' for newsreels and a call was made for vigorous action to protect such exhibitors. The biggest protest was to be made on behalf of the news theatres, not all of which were members of the CEA. The Chairman, R. H. Godfrey, is reported as saying: 'For ten years exhibitors have been clamouring for freedom in their bookings of newsreels, but they were warned that when contracts were cancelled there would be increases in prices. Despite that warning, the majority of exhibitors wanted to be released from this "dreadful contract".' Mr H. Pickering said: 'I have thrown out newsreels and my takings are going up. The till tells the tale—it never lies'. The newsreels were now including pictures of the 'Korean situation'. Kinemas opened to provide entertainment, not to make people miserable.

231   ANON. 'Eady Fund: newsreels stake a claim'. *Kinematograph Weekly*, (23 November 1950), p.7.

Newsreel theatres are anxious that newsreel companies should be able to recoup some of their increased expenses, which have caused them to put up the price of newsreels, from the money collected under the Eady scheme by the British Film Production Fund Ltd. The News and Specialised Theatre Association has asked the Fund to allocate some of its money for the newsreels. The news theatres hope to gain CEA support for their policy.

232   ANON. 'Granada project sidesteps newsreel issue: American news shots for Britain: sixty theatres showing *International Review*'. *Kinematograph Weekly*, (23 November 1950), p.3, 7.

At a time when the CEA is pressing the Newsreel Association to drop its cartel arrangement for increasing hire fees Granada has entered the newsreel business and this week the first edition of a new reel, *International Review*, has gone out to the sixty theatres on the circuit. The new reel is being produced from copies of *Telenews* which is controlled by the vast Hearst publishing organisation. The American originals are being flown to Britain and two issues combined into one weekly release. In addition to the American reels the Granada issue is being supplied with spot news coverage from the London bureau. The London Monseigneur news theatres are showing the reel under its American title and this may soon be changed to *International Review*. Some independent theatre owners are wondering if they could take up contracts for the British version at more equitable rates than those demanded by the British companies.

233   ANON. 'Bernstein denounces long-term news contracts: price is "immaterial".' *To-day's Cinema*, (28 November 1950), p.3, 8.

Reports Sidney Bernstein's views on the current newsreel dispute and on his own company's policy in regard to reels generally. Granada is interested in screen news and will show newsreels if they are good. Price is immaterial but it is wrong that exhibitors should be forced to contract for a minimum of six months as such a contract ignored possible deterioration in a particular newsreel service. An exhibitor might fairly be expected to book ahead for four weeks with a specific reel so as to permit the newsreel company adequate opportunity to plan for print supplies and the like. The material for Granada's *International Review* was being made up at British Movietonews.

234   ANON. 'Newsreel's decision for J. C. C.: "business relations in normal way".' *The Cinema*, (29 November 1950), p.3, 7.

Reports that the Newsreel Association Distribution Committee decision on the report of the Joint Consultative Committee on increased newsreel charges for news and specialised theatres will be sent to the Joint Committee for discussion at the next meeting. The Distribution Committee emphasises that the newsreel companies' business relationships with the average exhibitor are being carried on in the normal way. It is revealed that the CEA would accept the fact of a price schedule being in existence by 'recommendation' but they want the Newsreel Association resolution and the penalty clause for non-compliance rescinded. Newsreel executives, in the meantime, strongly oppose Mr Bernstein's view that exhibitors should be free to choose their reels and not be forced to contract for at least six months. They claim it would interfere with long-term planning.

235   ANON. 'Newsreels consider report by KRS on talks with CEA: "business relationship with average exhibitors continuing in normal way".' *Kinematograph Weekly*, (30 November 1950), p.7.

The distribution committee of the Newsreel Association emphasises that its business relationship with the average exhibitor is being carried on in the normal way. It has given consideration to the report submitted by the Kinematograph Renters' Society regarding the discussion which took place at the last meeting of the joint council relative to the newsreel theatre dispute. The distribution committee's decision in this matter will be conveyed to the general committee for discussion at its next meeting. The CEA minutes of the CEA-KRS meeting follows. Amongst arguments raised for the CEA it was pointed out that the real point at issue was the principle of a section, i.e. the specialised theatres, whose very existence depended upon obtaining a newsreel, being singled out for a fixed price. This section was not arguing on the prices of newsreels but on the principle that it was wrong for the Newsreel Association to fix a minimum price as an association with a penalty on its members.

236   ANON. 'The newsreel statement in full'. *To-day's Cinema*, (30 November 1950), p.5.

Prints the full statement issued by the Newsreel Association Distribution Committee after the Committee had received a report of a meeting of the Joint Consultative Committee on the newsreel dispute. Suggestions had been made that *The Cinema* of 29 November in extracting only parts of the statement had shown bias. The statement reads: 'As a result of its meeting today, the Distribution Committee of the Newsreel Association wish to emphasise that their business relationship with the average exhibitor is being carried on in the normal way. They have given consideration to the Report submitted by the President and Secretary of the K.R.S. regarding the discussion which took place at the last meeting of the J.C.C. relative to the Newsreel Theatre dispute. The Distribution Committee's decision in this matter will be conveyed to the Joint Committee for discussion at its next meeting and in the meantime they deprecate the ex-parte and 'inaccurate statements that have appeared in certain sections of the Trade Press. This is the only statement on this subject which the Newsreel Association or its members will make until after the matter has been further considered by the Joint Committee of the C.E.A. and K.R.S.'

237   ANON. 'A.C.T. jams BBC news: no seven-day week'. *Kinematograph Weekly*, (14 December 1950), p.122.

Action by the ACT is expected to prevent the BBC from putting out more than two issues of its television newsreel each week. The union has told Kay's West End laboratory, which handles the BBC processing, that it would be against the laboratory agreement with the union if the BBC is allowed processing facilities on seven days a week. The BBC has not been consulted by the union because it refuses to recognise the union. ACT members think it unfair that the BBC should have seven-day facilities when the commercial newsreels are restricted to five.

238   GEMMELL, Jock C. 'Newsreels'. *Kinematograph Weekly*, (14 December 1950), p.57.

In the column 'Technicians Report to the "Kine": ACT—from the inside' the author reports that the newsreel section of the Association has persistently exhorted the Newsreel Association to improve the quality of the newsreels 1) by producing longer reels, 2) by the abolition of the rota ('First-class camera work in competition is the basis of our business'.), and 3) by improving processing and consequently release to counter 'the serious challenge from television'. 'The solution is—COMPETENCE, COMPETITION and COLLABORATION'.

239　　ANON. 'Newsreel cartel dispute: CEA demands hearing by independent chairman—Hill: "Report first to KRS".' *Kinematograph Weekly*, (21 December 1950), p.3.

At a joint CEA-KRS discussion the previous Thursday the renters pointed out that the Newsreel Association had not yielded to the CEA point of view and after a lengthy discussion the CEA delegates formally pointed out that they must insist on an independent chairman. Frank Hill, secretary of the KRS, has said that no action following the CEA request can be taken until the matter has been reported back to the KRS council.

240　　ANON. 'KRS demands 50 p.c. ceiling arbitration: surprise move in newsreel talks'. *Kinematograph Weekly*, (28 December 1950), p.3, 7.

The Kinematograph Renters' Society has demanded an independent arbitrator to decide whether or not the Cinematograph Exhibitors' Association is right in operating a 50 percent ceiling recommendation on film rentals in general. The Newsreel Association saw no reason why a revision of the price schedule that had been in existence for newsreels for over thirty years should be discussed with the CEA. If an arbitrator were appointed he could be informed that there were two price schedules in dispute. It was the KRS intention to place on the agenda for the next meeting of the Joint Committee the question of the 50 percent maximum, and it was therefore not prepared to accept arbitration on the Newsreel Association matter until after the next meeting of the Joint Committee, nor to have the 50 percent maximum matter treated as merely subsidiary.

1951

241　　BUCHANAN, Andrew. *Going to the cinema*. London: Phoenix House, 1951. viii, 160p. ('Excursions' series for young people).

Chapter 6, 'News reels of to-day and to-morrow', p.98–113, discusses the newsreel under the following headings: 'Are you interested in the news reel?—The news reel does not explain—What *IS* news?—Sometimes a one-sided affair—News reels don't tell the whole story—Speed the essence of the news reel—Rain, hail or snow: the camera must turn—The news reel library of noises—Something more than a news reel (*March of Time* and *This Modern Age*)—Will the news reel change?—A news reel that would tell you why'.

242　　ANON. 'Newsreel price issue is unique problem'. *The Cinema*, (17 January 1951), p.3.

Referring to the suggested arbitration on the newsreel dispute, E. J. Hinge, CEA National Treasurer is quoted as telling Northern branch members: 'I deplore the fact that for the first time since the establishment of the J.C.C. we have come across a problem which we have not been able to solve'. He could not understand why the KRS felt it was for the good of the industry that any section of their members should impose a penalty clause. 'That is our principal objection in this issue. We are not standing for an innovation like that. It would create a price ring of the most vicious nature'.

243　　ANON. 'News theatre rating plea succeeds: TV blamed for loss of popularity'. *Kinematograph Weekly*, (1 February 1951), p.9.

News theatres were losing popularity all over the country due to the shortage of money and the effects of television it was stated at an enquiry in Sheffield on the previous Friday when Sheffield Corporation objections to a £355 reduction from £1,135 in the gross rating assessment of the News Theatre, Fitzalan Square, Sheffield were dismissed by the local valuation court. Also, the news theatre was off the main street of shopping traffic. 'Ideally it should be sited in a busy shopping centre, recognised amusement place, or near a main-line station'. The gross value was assessed at £800, the figure agreed by the Inland Revenue authorities.

244   GORDON, Kenneth. 'Forty years with a newsreel camera'. *The Cine-Technician*, vol. 17, no. 89 (March-April 1951), p.44–50.

Recalls episodes in newsreel history with an anecdotal account of the author's own experiences in peace and wartime (Balkan War, First World War, Irish War of Independence) and of the newsreel men he worked with. Note: This is a revised and extended version of the lecture given to the BKS on 5 April 1950. (Reported in the BKS Journal, vol. 17, no. 2, August 1950 p.47–50.)

245   ANON. 'Newsreels get the "blues" after TV: increased stock costs may force some out of business: exhibitor resistance is increasing'. *Kinematograph Weekly*, (29 March 1951), p.3, 6.

Newsreel executives are holding conferences to meet those threats that may force at least one reel out of business and cause others to amalgamate, 1) the increase in cost of positive stock when the new safety stock comes into general supply, 2) the continued improvement in the BBC television programmes 'which reached a climax this weekend when TV transmissions were made of the Boat Race to viewers all over the Southern half of the British Isles,' and 3) strong exhibitor resistance to increased rentals, with many independents dropping contracts or taking other reels on subsequent runs.

246   ANON. 'In the House: Government should not dictate contents of newsreels—Gordon Walker'. *Kinematograph Weekly*, (9 August 1951), p.9.

Briefly reports the view expressed by the Minister for Commonwealth Relations, who also did not consider that it would be suitable for the Central Office of Information to start newsreel distribution, in reply to a question from Ian Mikardo about the monopoly aspect of the dispute between the Newsreel Association and the *International Review* concerning films taken by the Anglo-Iranian Oil Company.

1952

247   BAECHLEIN, Peter, and MULLER-STRAUSS, Maurice. *Newsreels across the world*. Paris: Unesco, 1952. 100p.

The only study of the structural and financial aspects of the newsreels. International coverage. Includes also a section on television newsreels. There are many references to the U.K. e.g., pages 38–39 tables an analysis of items about the United Kingdom which were included in the United States newsreels during the 10-month period 1 January–31 October 1949, and pages 68–69 has a section on some British cinemagazines, including children's cinemagazines.

1953

248   REISZ, Karel. *The technique of film editing*. London: Focal Press, 1953. 285p.

Chapter 12, p.184–193, deals with the planning and editing of the newsreel. (The Chapter is repeated in the 2nd edition edited by Reisz and Gavin Millar in 1968.)

249   ANON. 'Warner-Color is choice for big Pathé film: Sir Philip Warter reveals Coronation plans: over 200 copies to service Britain'. *The Cinema*, (28 January 1953), p.3, 24.

Already in production, the film is to be entitled 'Elizabeth is Queen' and will be produced by Howard Thomas and distributed by Associated-British Pathé. It will be approximately one hour in length and will be trade shown on the Friday following Tueday's Coronation ceremony. Over 200 copies will service A.B.-Pathé's first-run customers throughout Great Britain on Monday, 8th June. Dupe-negatives will be flown to America from which prints will be taken to service that country. Copies of the film will also be flown to the English-speaking British Dominions. Howard Thomas added: 'We shall have commentators and they will be well-known artistes, but they won't be billed. Having reviewed pictures of the last Coronation, I believe there was far too great an emphasis on the commentators, far too much talk and too little reliance placed on the spectacular pageantry of the occasion'.

250   ANON. 'First stereo newsreel is screened'. *Kinematograph Weekly*, (9 April 1953), p.6.

Reports the screening in three of London's news theatres of the first 3-D newsreel to be released in Britain—'London Tribute', a record of the funeral of Queen Mary, made by the company, Sterio-Techniques. Just over 300 feet in length it is in black and white. The sequence begins at Windsor Castle, then moves to Marlborough House and shots of the funeral procession taken from Admiralty Arch, ending with a shot of the Embankment at night.

251   ANON. 'Newsreels all set to beat television competition: BKS told of 3-D and colour plans'. *Kinematograph Weekly*, (9 April 1953), p.7.

Reports the statement made by Howard Thomas, Executive Producer of *Pathé News* that large-screen television, 3-D and colour are the weapons with which the film industry will fight the competition of the television newsreel. Television is the real competitor and competition will be enhanced if sponsored television follows. The telefilm is another weapon of TV. Newsreels must compete by offering shots beyond the scope of TV. The Coronation will be filmed in black and white, colour and 3-D colour.

252   BOWMAN, Gerald. 'News of the Coronation colour film plans'. *The Evening News* (London), (6 May 1953), p.9.

Brief item giving 'the first detailed news' of the only full-length colour film of the Coronation, 'A Queen is Crowned', to be made by Castleton-Knight with commentary by Sir Lawrence Olivier from a script by Christopher Fry.

253   HARMAN, Jympson. 'A hundred cameras will be turning, and then begins the rush to the screen'. *The Evening News* (London), (28 May 1953), p.4.

Outlines how the newsreels will be covering the Coronation—the cameras manned by teams of three, with a policeman seconded to each so that the motor-cyclists can rush the cans of film to the labs: the rush to process the films and edit them; the worldwide distribution by air of the finished product. Two feature-length colour films are being made, "A Queen is Crowned" (by Castleton-Knight) and "Elizabeth is Queen" (by Howard Thomas for Pathé). First copies are expected in the West End on the Friday after Tuesday, 2nd June.

254   HARMAN, Jympson. 'Coronation in colour: three versions of the day'. *The Evening News* (London) (6 June 1953), p.4.

Reviews the three newsreel films of the Coronation, "A Queen is Crowned", "Elizabeth is Queen", and the shorter (20 min.) "Coronation Day", made by British Movietone (with commentary read by James McKechnie from a script by Gerald Sanger). Also discusses the BBC television coverage.

255   ANON. 'Wake up, newsreel men! Endorsing Jympson Harman's recent plea [in the *Evening News*] for longer newsreels, "Newshawk" hits hard at newsreel executives and technicians for their "do-nothing" policy'. *The Cine-Technician: Journal of the Association of Cine-Technicians*, vol. 19, no. 104 (August 1953), p.95.

The short 700-foot newsreel continues because production costs have enormously risen. The demand for longer reels, however, already exists. Despite the serious competition of TV the short reel is still very popular. Exhibitors who experimentally dropped newsreels out of their programmes last time the price was put up have mostly abandoned the experiment because the customers objected to a show without news. Exhibitors' reluctance to pay more for a longer newsreel can be broken down by propaganda. The propaganda should point out that if the present short reel is popular how much more so would be the longer reel. Much newsreel reporting is thrown away by its very shortness. 'Indeed, many stories nowadays can be missed altogether if someone passes in front of you on the way to a seat'. It is instructive to see how attentively the audience responds when big news forces editors to devote 400-500 feet to a subject. The rationing of positive stock is still a formidable obstacle to be overcome. The ACT Newsreel Section failed to persuade the Board of Trade to meet it on that issue four years ago; but there has since been a change of government, many restrictions have gone and a new approach by a deputation 'carefully leaving our Communist members at home', might produce the necessary stock. Apathy on the part of newsreel executives is another handicap. The newsreel of the future must be in colour. Colour is even more important to newsreels than to features. In every kind of quality the newsreel can beat TV, which is often tedious and as yet shows no signs of understanding the needs of a daily issue, but it cannot match the TV time factor, unless it evolves a new technique. Looking into the future the newsreel's hope lies in magnetic recording.

1954

256   DUNCAN, Charles. *A photographic pilgrim's progress: being the adventures of an itinerant photographer among cameras, cabbages and kings*. London: Focal Press, 1954. viii, 155p.

Chapter 16, p.102–109 relates how Duncan and James Scott Brown filmed the Coronation of George V in 1910.

1955

257   BRITISH BROADCASTING CORPORATION. *BBC Handbook 1955*. London: BBC, 1955. 224p.

'News broadcasts', p.51–53, includes two brief paragraphs on the BBC *Television Newsreel* (p.53): 'The presentation of topical items in visual form was developed for some five years in *Television Newsreel*, which occupied about a quarter of an hour and appeared latterly on five nights a week, with a composite week-end edition. It was produced by a special unit of the Television Film Department, which supplied most of the material. The News Division (which always had a member of its staff associated with the old 'Newsreel') and the Television Service are now developing a combined news and newsreel programme which is televised nightly for fifteen minutes and includes pictorial material of various kinds, drawn from many different sources. *News and Newsreel*, inaugurated in July 1954, aims at giving the public in the United Kingdom as comprehensive an illustrated service of news as is possible within the limitations imposed by the existing sources of illustration and their availability. It is hoped that eventually this service will be the equal in scope of that which has been given in sound for many years'.

258   NOBLE, Ronnie. *Shoot first! Assignments of a newsreel cameraman.* London: Harrap, 1955. 271p.

An anecdotal account of the cameraman's assignments at home, and abroad e.g., Europe, the Middle East and Far East covering World War 2 and the Korean War. Includes a chapter, 'The Newsreel War', covering the newsreel companies' pinching activities during the period of competition for exclusive rights.

259   ELTON, Sir Arthur. 'The film as source material for history'. *Aslib Proceedings*, vol. 7, no. 4 (November 1955), p.207–39.

The President of the Scientific Film Association and Chairman of Film Centre Ltd., bases his text substantially on a paper he delivered at the Aslib Annual Conference at Blackpool on 24 September 1955. Films, by which he means essentially actuality films, can be used, as other historical source material can be used, for various and different historical purposes. 'For at least the first thirty years the content of the newsreels was determined mainly by the passing fads and fancies of the time. The reels were there to entertain, and serious topics were usually either treated unseriously or avoided. Of scenes of one-legged men pushing turnips with their noses from Paris to Rome there is much . . . but of industry, technology, sociology, art, poetry, agriculture, only accidental glimpses . . . There are notable exceptions to this story'. Points out that 'some of the early newsreel companies kept their files intact, and there are a few nearly unbroken runs stretching back from today to the early nineteen-hundreds'. With World War 2 there came a change in the content of the reels as film poured in from the Service Film Units and the newsreel cameramen. Goes on to discuss documentary film, matters of preservation, the BBC *Television Newsreel* and the libraries of the newsreel companies.

1956

260   ANON. 'Newsreels hit by TV: counter publicity given in papers'. *To-day's Cinema*, (24 May 1956), p.3, 8.

Briefly reports opinions voiced at the previous day's meeting of the Sussex C.E.A. Considerable loss of business was reported during the BBC's screening of the film 'Stage Coach'. Newsreels are now a farce because of TV. Even the Cup Final was covered before it could reach the cinema screens. Advance TV publicity in the Press is blamed.

1957

261   BRITISH BROADCASTING CORPORATION. *BBC Handbook 1957.* London: BBC, 1957. 288p.

'News broadcasts', p.62–66 includes the following note in the Television section (p.66): 'Following the development of news film sources, the first full fifteen-minute illustrated *News Bulletin* was introduced in the Television Service in the late summer of 1955. This replaced the combined programme *News and Newsreel*. At the same time a Newsreel was introduced on five days of the week and an illustrated News Summary every day'.

1958

262   ANON. 'Weekly reel with colour to replace *GB/Universal News*: news magazine (about 1,000 ft.) which will have "more lasting impact".' *Daily Cinema*, (19 November 1958), p.1.

The Rank Organisation announces rationalisation, with two newsreels—*Gaumont-British News* and *Universal News*—disappearing to make way for one reel produced once instead of twice a week. The new reel, produced mainly in Eastman colour will contain from one to three stories per issue and is scheduled to begin early in the New Year. While there will be considerable emphasis on topicality the aim will be to present an entertainment reel 'which will have a more lasting impact than the present ephemeral newsreel content'.

1959

263   WYAND, Paul. *Useless if delayed*. London: Harrap, 1959. 256p.

An anecdotal account of the cameraman's assignments at home and abroad, with a chapter on pirating and extensive coverage of his wartime activities. In all, the cameraman went on 5,206 assignments.

264   ANON. 'Newsreels must justify Levy share, say MPs'. *Kinematograph Weekly*, (5 November 1959), p.3.

Reports that the newsreel companies would receive a new source of revenue—a share of the Levy—as a result of being included in the Quota under the Films Bill which was being debated in the Commons that day. MPs however felt that they should raise their standards and provide livelier and better material to justify 'this financial first-aid'. Labour MPs especially were lukewarm about the change, some believing that newsreels were on the way out anyway because television could do their job better and faster.

1962

265   ANON. 'CEA propose grant for newsreels: AIC urges "no discrimination".' *Daily Cinema*, (19 November 1962), p.3, 8.

Reports a CEA and AIC (Association of Independent Cinemas) recommendation to the Board of Trade that British newsreels should qualify for some form of Exchequer grant as their sale abroad contributed to British prestige.

1963

266   SWEENY, W. H. O. 'Technical requirements for a television news service: an address to the British Kinematograph Society on Wednesday, November 21st 1962'. *British Kinematography*, vol. 42, no. 2 (February 1963), p.42–53.

The author, Chief Engineer of Independent Television News, explains the philosophy underlying the planning of the complex installation considered essential for the assembly and transmission of a ten-minute news bulletin of film stories broken up by shots of a newscaster in the studio under the following headings: The Film Camera Section, Mobility, Lighting, Cameramen and Preparation of Material, Transfer Facilities, Sound Reproducers, Recording, Portable Tape Recorders, Telecine, Operational Method, Control Routing, Stories from Other Stations, Telstar and Other Remote Sources, The News Studio, Studio

Lighting, Studio Cameras—Captions, Tele-prompting, Positional Flexibility, Backing and Sets, Tonal Balance, Backings of Various Types, Sound Equipment, Control Rooms, Inter-Communications, Sound Control, Camera Control, Lighting Controls, Commentaries, Central Apparatus Room, Routing, Importance of Ventilation for Apparatus, Telerecording Maintenance Facilities, The Future. Finishes with details of the discussion.

267   GILL, Alan. 'The story of the newsreels. Part 1: Buccaneering days'. *Amateur Cine World*, vol. 6, no. 2 (11 July 1963), p.70–71, 86.

At a time when only two of the old newsreels, *Pathé News* and *British Movietone News* are still in existence the article, taken from the reminiscences of newsreel cameramen and reporters, past and present, highlights some of the more colourful and amusing incidents in the story of the British newsreels.

268   GILL, Alan. 'The story of the newsreels. Part 2: Television takes over'. *Amateur Cine World*, vol. 6, no. 3 (18 July 1963), p.110–111.

Anecdotes of the newsreel cameramen in wartime. After the war the cameramen returned to the rivalry of former years though 'pinching', 'snatching', or 'pirating' had largely disappeared. The advent of television newsreels saw the gradual death of the old ways and the birth of a new and very different brand of film journalism. 'With television newsreels, the emphasis is on reporting and direct questioning rather than mere film recording'. Anecdotes of the early activities of television newsreel cameramen.

1965

269   *National Film Archive Catalogue. Part 1: Silent News Films 1895–1933.* 2nd Edition. London: British Film Institute, 1965. vi, 308p.

Lists material from Warwick, Eclair, Gaumont, Pathé, *Topical Budget*, *Empire News Bulletin* and others.

1967

270   HUNNINGS, Neville March. *Film censors and the law.* London: Allen & Unwin, 1967. 474p.

Chapter 3, 'Extension and consolidation of control (1925–1955)', Section (e), 'Press shows and newsreels', p.109–113, looks particularly at the efforts made by the County Councils to impose some form of censorship on the newsreels, which were in an exposed position because 'they were completely unprotected by the law'.

1969

271   HOPKINSON, Peter. *Split focus: an involvement in two decades.* London: Rupert Hart-Davis, 1969. 224p.

The author, who served with the Army Film and Photographic Unit during World War 2, describes how he covered events in theatres of war in Europe and Asia. In 1946 he joined the *March of Time* as a roving cameraman-reporter.

1970

272   GAY, Ken. 'The lone newsreel'. *Films & Filming*, vol. 16, no. 7 (April 1970), p.88.

Mentions the activities of the last of the British reels, *British Movietone News*, still offering large-screen actuality news as something better than television and maintaining six camera teams to prove it. Emphasises the importance of the newsreel library. The main section of the article deals with the preservation of historical film material, including documentary.

1971

273   NORMAN, Philip. 'The newsreel boys'. *The Sunday Times Magazine*, (10 January 1971), cover + p.8–15.

A detailed and affectionate history of the activities of the 'fun-filled, large-overcoated and bibulous men with loud voices and connections as close to the music hall as to any technical union'—the newsreel cameramen. 'In the service of the five newsreel emblems—Pathé's cockerel, Movietone's scroll, Gaumont's town crier, Universal's globe and Paramount's 'Eyes and Ears of the World'—they did the most splendid, appalling things'. The activities of the editors, in particular L. Castleton-Knight, Tommy Cummins and Kenneth Gordon and, to a lesser degree, the commentators are also covered. There are some excellent photographs.

274   PRONAY, Nicholas. 'British newsreels in the 1930s: 1. Audience and producers'. *History*, vol. 56 (October 1971), p.411–18.

As sources of primary information about the events they portrayed the newsreels are only of peripheral value. As records of what the public was told about the events they are of historical importance and utility: it is in the size, social composition and the attitudes of the *audience* that the strongest case for studying the newsreels is to be found. Soundtracks enabled the newsreels not only to show something but to interpret it. Beginning with S. Rowson's statistical survey of the cinema industry (1934) the author goes on to discuss other relevant surveys, e.g., the Social Survey of Merseyside which was carried out about the same time. It is important to see figures for cinema attendance in comparison with the penetration of the newspapers and radio. The newsreel industry was a very large industry, e.g., the five newsreel companies were producing between them by 1933 an average of 520 newsreel per annum. Some of them also produced a weekend edition and they all produced occasional special editions. The structure of the industry ensured that it would model itself on the popular press. Goes on to discuss editorial policy and the news coverage of the reels. Points out that as prints were very expensive and accounted for much of the companies' budget only about one third of the cinemas received a print of the reels when they were issued. These first-run houses showed the print for three days, then passed it on to the next rung down the ladder until, in about three weeks, the newsreel worked its way down its appointed circuit.

1972

275   PRONAY, Nicholas, SMITH, Betty R. and HASTIE, Tom. *The use of film in history teaching*. London: Historical Association, 1972. 35p.

A section of Chapter 1: 'The use of film in history teaching' by Nicholas Pronay, p.9–13, looks at the way 'the technological complexities of film reportage affected in two important aspects the way in which the news was gathered and presented'. They affected editorial policy and because of the camera equipment, the way a story was covered. Goes on to outline how a film crew and its sound team would have covered a mass meeting. Points out that newsfilm is not some unadulterated truth about the past untouched by the distortions of human interpretation. Suggests how newsreels can be used in teaching.

(276) PRONAY, Nicholas. 'British newsreels in the 1930s: 2. Their policies and impact'. *History*, vol. 57, no. 189 (February 1972), p.63–72.

For all the apparent competition between the newsreel companies there was little difference between them in matters of editorial policy. The five Editors met regularly to decide on their policies concerning 'touchy' subjects and they abided by the agreements. One fundamental difference distinguished newsreels from newspapers—the general unsureness whether to extend to newsreels the traditionally accepted norm of the freedom of the press or whether to place them under the traditionally accepted norm of the lack of freedom of the stage. There was great sensitivity about the presentation of *any* political issue through the medium of film. The contemporaries of the newsreels regarded the cinema as an exceptionally potent means of communication—and of propaganda for that reason—with the result that the newsreels had to evolve an entirely different pattern of behaviour from the newspapers. While the newsreels infuriated the cognoscenti and were contemptuously ignored by the educated classes in general, their consensual approach and their years of learning about the tastes of the average man, allowed them to build up a capital of trust which stood them, and the country, in good stead from 1939 to the end of the war. It allowed them to 'editorialise' freely when the BBC could not. The most intractable problem about the newsreels as a medium of communication is the question of how their effect on their huge and regular public can be assessed. There is little doubt that they 'got through' to their working-class audience. Goes on to discuss the difference between reading a newspaper and viewing a newsreel constructed to move as fast as possible. Underlines the value to the reels of their film, essentially stock-shot, libraries. The combination of live shots with stock shots and live sound with stock sound was the essence of the newsreel. Because yesterday's *issue* was tomorrow's library footage, the newsreels' preservation by their owners in unbroken series enhances their usefulness. They constitute important historical evidence which deserves study.

1973

277 PONTECORVO, Lisa. 'Aspects of documentary and newsreel research'. *Archive Film Compilation Booklet*, Bletchley: Open University Press, 1973. p.6–14.

Section 1, p.6–9 discusses the development of cinema reportage. Section 2, p.9–12, the origins of the newsreel—French, British, German and Russian. Section 3, 'Finding the film', p.12–14, outlines some of the problems and pitfalls of researching newsreel footage.

278 ALDGATE, Anthony. 'British newsreels and the Spanish Civil War'. *Film & History*, vol. 3, no. 1 (February 1973), p.1–8, 16.

The newsreels in Britain were not officially subject to censorship but this did not mean that they were exempt from pressures of the public or governmental varieties. Using as an example coverage of the Spanish Civil War, with additional reference to the War in Abyssinia, the author examines the unofficial censorship of the newsreels by the Home Office (through its 'Model Conditions'), the County Councils Association and public opinion. Also discusses the question of pro-rebel political bias in coverage of the Spanish conflict.

279 ALDGATE, Anthony. 'British newsreels and the Spanish Civil War'. *History*, vol. 58 (1973), p.60–3.

From a general 'war is horrible' posture the British newsreels took on in their coverage of the Spanish conflict a decidedly political bias, a pro-rebel bias. Such bias also manifested itself by the sin of omission. The thesis is discussed giving examples of particular stories.

1974

280   ALDGATE, Anthony. 'The production of "Spanish Civil War". Part 1: The Archives and the newsreels'. *University Vision*, no. 11 (April 1974), p.16–23.

The director/editor of the InterUniversity History Film Consortium production describes the newsreel sources he researched for material for inclusion in the compilation film. Makes the point that *Universal Talking News* was quickly discarded because of its generally poor coverage of foreign events, and adds: 'Universal was financially the poor cousin of the newsreel industry in the thirties, though, according to some sources, at one point during this period it had the highest circulation, simply because it reached a great many of the independent cinemas up and down the country . . .' *Gaumont-British News* (which, according to June 1936 figures circulated in 1,750 cinemas throughout the British Isles) and *British Paramount News* were far better endowed. Goes on to discuss newsreel production techniques including commentating, and some of the stories of the Spanish War which he viewed. (Part 2 of this article, 'A Film in the Making', *University Vision*, no. 12, December 1974, p.42–49; describes how the material selected was incorporated in the compilation film.)

1975

281   BEATTIE, Alan, DILKS, David and PRONAY, Nicholas. *Neville Chamberlain*. InterUniversity History Film Consortium, 1975. 22p. (Archive series no. 1).

Booklet which accompanies film of the same title. Discusses the role of the newsreels in the thirties before going on to introduce the newsreel extracts used in the film. Sets the context of the speeches and considers Chamberlain's speaking style.

282   THORPE, Frances, ed. *A directory of British film and television libraries*. London: Slade Film History Register, 1975. 55p.

A survey of the main existing sources in Britain of film which records aspects of the history and sociology of the twentieth century. The articles on the eight sources are written by the custodians of the collections. In addition there is an article by the editor on the methodology of the research undertaken by the Slade Film History Register on the British newsreels and, a translation from the French of the article, 'A new source of history: creation of an archive of historical cinematography', by the Pole, B. Matuszewski, published in Paris in 1898.

1976

283   ALDGATE, Anthony. *The use of film as a historical source: British newsreels and the Spanish Civil War*. University of Edinburgh, PhD thesis (1976).

284   BARNES, John. *The beginnings of the cinema in England*. Newton Abbot: David & Charles, 1976. 240p.

Explores in depth the progress made in the field of cinematography until the end of 1896. Appendix 1, p.201–219, lists British films made in 1895–96, most of which are 'topical' films.

285   BAWDEN, Liz-Anne. (ed.) *The Oxford companion to film*. London: OUP, 1976. xii, 767p.

Pages 500–502 contain a brief international history of the newsreel by Helen P. Harrison.

286   BOYLE, Peter G. *The origins of the Cold War*. InterUniversity History Film Consortium, 1976. 16p. (Archive series no. 2).

Booklet which accompanies film of the same title. Discusses newsreel coverage of the Cold War and introduces the extracts used in the film.

287   PRONAY, Nicholas. 'The newsreels: the illusion of actuality'. *The historian and film*, edited by Paul Smith. Cambridge: CUP, 1976. p.95–119.

The history of the news film falls into three periods: 1895–6 to 1910, the birth of the cinema which already covered topical items to the introduction of the first regular weekly newsreels: 1910–1928, the age of the silent newsreel, during which the structure of the elaborate international newsreel organisations was fully evolved and the newsreel's potential political significance foreshadowed: 1927–1950s which began with the introduction of sound newsreels and ended with the supplanting of the reels by television news. The author first surveys the international scene covering organisation, production techniques and distribution, then considers the effect on the newsreels of World War 1. Goes on to discuss the developments of the British sound reels. Stresses the importance of the film library to the newsreel company. Newly established newsreels had virtually no chance of competing without a library. Discusses the content of the reels, trivia and stunts as against serious items. Finds there is evidence to suggest that one is dealing with a medium which had a lot to say and in an exceptionally direct and persuasive way to that very large and particularly susceptible portion of the public which went to the cinemas. Concludes with the effect on the reels of World War 2 and the aftermath which saw them succumb to television.

288   ALDGATE, Anthony. 'Newsreel scripts: a case-study'. *History*, vol. 61 (1976), p.390–92.

The interest shown by historians in cinema newsreels as a primary source for historical study has centred upon the actual newsreel issues, as they would have been shown in the cinemas, with particular regard being given to the individual stories which make up these issues. It should not be forgotten, however, that the spoken commentary to an individual story generally went through several drafts before being finally accepted and laid over the edited film. Examines scripts written by E. V. H. Emmett, editor and commentator of *Gaumont-British News* for three stories about British prisoners, members of the International Brigade, held in Franco's detention camps. Gaumont was a company of decidedly Conservative sympathies and a bias in the presentation of the subject matter is detected.

289   KUEHL, Jerry. '"Film as Evidence"—a review'. *History Workshop*, no. 2 (Autumn 1976), p.135–139.

A lengthy review of the BBC-2 series of five programmes, 'Film as Evidence'. Begins by stating the author's opinion—'the series (does) not help viewers to evaluate films critically. How (can) it? Its commentary (is) misleading and often simply wrong. Its use of film (is) slovenly and sometimes less than scrupulous'. Takes issue with the four assumptions that underpin the first programme, namely, 1) newsreels were unknown before the 1930s; 2) some fifteen million people went to the cinema to see them each week; 3) newsreels were the principle source of information about the world outside their immediate surroundings for those fifteen million people; and 4) cinemagoers believed what they were told by newsreel commentaries. The reviewer finds all claims unjustified because 1) newsreels were an integral part of cinema programmes before the First World War; 2) there is no evidence that audiences went to the cinema in order to see the *newsreels*; rather they went to see the *programme*; 3) the suggestion that the newsreels were the principal source of information ignores the newspapers and radio, and 4) no serious studies of audience reactions to newsreels were ever made. Goes on to take issue with the physical quality of the films in the series, some of the cutting, the commentary on the Suez programme and the portrayal of Neville Chamberlain as the first political leader to understand the potentialities of the mass media and to use them to propel himself to political dominance. Concludes that the series makes its points by showing films at the wrong speed, with sound and music improperly added and without identification, and passes off as authentic original material which has been re-cut. In addition, the commentary makes its points in the same style as the newsreel commentaries which it pillories.

1977

290   BRITISH UNIVERSITIES FILM COUNCIL. *The Slade Film History Register: report of a working party to consider the future development of the Slade Film History Register.* London: British Universities Film Council, 1977. 37p.

The report summarises the work of the Register, in particular its work in indexing and classifying selected stories from British newsreel collections, from its inception in 1969 at the Slade School of Fine Art to its transfer to the BUFC in 1975. A working party was then convened to review the function of the Register and make recommendations for possible future development. The report discusses the advantages and scope of a central register of film and television materials and makes recommendations on the preservation of and access to the collections. The appendices list the newsreel issue sheets held in the Register and suggest ways in which the contents of the newsreels might be indexed.

291   SMITH, Howard. Letters to the Editor. *History Workshop*, no. 3 (Spring 1977), p.195–97.

The producer of 'Film as Evidence' totally refutes Jerry Kuehl's review in *History Workshop*, no. 2. Among the points he rejects are: the suggestion that the physical quality of Programme 1 was due to copying from low-quality videotape recordings; that some of the excerpts shown were from British, some from German newsreels (all were British as the whole point of the series was to show British newsreels as they were seen by the British people at that time); that two separate stories on the liberation of Belsen had been cut together (the story shown was one Gaumont story). The author also challenges Mr Kuehl's suppositions about Programme 1—the commentary did not make the points the reviewer questioned or at least phrase them in the terms assumed: there is not a single case where he reports accurately what the film actually said or showed and where he has his own historical facts right. Challenges Mr Kuehl to say how he would have approached the perennial problem of presenting silent film on television.

292   KUEHL, Jerry. 'Riposte (to Howard Smith's letter)'. *History Workshop*, no. 3 (Spring 1977), p.197–99.

Refutes in turn many of the points made by Howard Smith in the same issue of *History Workshop*. He finds Mr Smith's defence of his reliance on Visnews material only for the series unconvincing, repeats his objections to what he considers to be poor quality videotape copied from videotape transfers, raises questions about step printing, gives his ideas about the presentation of silent film on television and repeats his assertion about the Belsen story in greater detail. With regard to the commentary he claims he was not talking about *lines* of commentary but about the assumptions underlying them.

293   LEWIS, Jonathan. 'Before hindsight'. *Sight & Sound*, vol. 46, no. 2 (Spring 1977), p.68–73.

Examines the attitudes expressed by the British newsreels toward the events that led to the Second World War. Regarding Germany a huge factor that had to be borne in mind was that from 1933 onwards all film coming out of that country was filmed for propaganda purposes under the control of Dr Goebbels. The British newsreels, thus, had to rely on what they were sent. The author and his colleagues in their researches found 'only about 1,000 items which concerned aspects of Anglo-German political relationships between 1930 and 1939', a figure which represents about one fiftieth of the total newsreel output of the period. The effects of editorial policy and censorship on the newsreels (with particular reference to the *British Paramount News* issue of 22 September 1938) and the attitudes of left-wing film-makers are discussed.

294   ALDGATE, Anthony. '1930s newsreels: censorship & controversy'. *Sight & Sound*, vol. 46, no. 3 (Summer 1977), p.154–57.

Though often accused of triviality the British newsreels were considered capable of dealing with straight news: the various attempts to censor them provide adequate evidence of how seriously they were taken in the thirties in some quarters. The author examines the unofficial pressures that were brought to bear on the newsreel companies giving specific examples of offending stories, in particular the *British Paramount News* deletion of items from its issue of 22 September 1938 during the Munich crisis, which led to heated debate in the House of Commons. Concludes that the spectre of censorship or of public and governmental pressure haunted the 1930s. The newsreels simply had to learn to live with it. On a more general level it is possible to see the years from 1933 to 1939 as leading quite logically and cumulatively towards the kind of government control that manifested itself during World War 2.

295   HONRI, Baynham. 'Newsreel boys' reunion'. *Screen International*, no. 91 (11 June 1977), p.10–11.

Reports on a reunion of newsreel cameramen and sound-men at Samuelson's 'Southern Lighting' premises. Out of 110 veterans invited 80 were able to attend.

296   PRONAY, Nicholas. Letters to the Editor. *History Workshop*, no. 4 (Autumn 1977), p.252–53.

Takes issue with Jerry Kuehl's 'Riposte' to Howard Smith in the previous issue of *History Workshop*, in particular with the allegation that there had been improper interference with the historical principles on which the selection of newsreel items shown was based, and with the misrepresentation of the relationship between him, as historian for two programmes in the series, and the producer. He had chosen Gaumont-British rather than any other newsreel as the central thread for Programmes 1 & 5 because this emerged as substantially the most widely seen newsreel in working-class cinemas and because it was also, taking the 1930s as a whole, the most popular in absolute terms. He also challenges Kuehl's assumptions about evidence of the cinema-going habits of the public in the Thirties.

297   LEWIS, Jonathan. Letter to *Sight & Sound*, vol. 46, no. 4 (Autumn 1977), p.262.

Queries an assumption in Anthony Aldgate's article on the censorship of newsreels in the 1930s in the previous issue of *Sight & Sound* about the *British Paramount News* issue of 22 September 1938. Writes: 'although one can ascertain from the script that the whole (Wickham Steed) speech was not used even before the reel was withdrawn, one cannot tell why'. Hence, one 'cannot assume that political expediency was the sole or even the strongest influence on the 30s newsreels'.

298   WEGG-PROSSER, Victoria. 'The Archive of the Film and Photo League'. *Sight & Sound*, vol. 46, no. 4 (Autumn 1977), p.245–47.

Discusses the history and output of the League including *Workers' Topical News* and *Workers' Newsreel*.

1978

299   HULBERT, J. C. *The British Cinema newsreels' treatment of the British military, 1948–1960*. University of Keele, MA thesis (1978).

300   PRONAY, Nicholas. '"Before Hindsight": a review'. *BUFC Newsletter*, no. 35 (November 1978), p.19–22.

The film, primarily an examination of the role of the newsreels, recognises that the evidentiary value of the reels lies as much in their sound-tracks, what they said, as in the photographic records which they preserve. The reviewer takes issue with the film-makers over their interpretation of the *British Paramount News* reel reporting the introduction of conscription in Germany and the *Gaumont-British News* reel on the re-occupation of the Rhinelands. Goes on: 'Alas, other examples could be cited from throughout the film casting serious doubts on the credentials of the arguments it presents and on the useability of the film in education. The most valuable parts of the film, and one does wonder what may have been cut out from those as well, are the statements made by Gerald Sanger and Leslie Mitchell, respectively editor and commentator of Movietone'. Rather than presenting 'an analysis of the newsreels as *films* by men of the cinema' the film sets out to provide a history of the policy of Appeasement as applied in the case of Germany in the 1930s. However, the history purveyed by the film is ill-informed. The trouble is that 'the selection of (the newsreel) items appears to have been motivated by some rather strange criteria'.

301   SMITH, Howard. '"Something has to be done": a note on research in cinema newsreels'. *BUFC Newsletter*, no. 35 (November 1978), p.16, 18.

Discusses the problems involved in researching for a 25 minute film showing the value of newsreels as historical evidence, e.g., not all the evidence has survived—virtually all the commentaries of the issues of *British Paramount News* have been destroyed; *Gaumont-British News* once 'the most influential of all British cinema newsreels' becomes so bland after 1945 that, with a few outstanding exceptions, it is virtually impossible to use it as evidence of any attitude at all. Points out the constraints imposed by the 25 minute duration in selecting material to build up a picture of a gradual change in attitudes: one first selects material judged to be the most typical and then chooses extracts from that material. The question of narrative links follows. Goes on to discuss the British newsreel coverage of denazification and the re-establishment of political life in defeated Germany. Note: 'Something has to be done' is one of the films in the BBC-2 series 'Film as Evidence' (1976), and deals with the way events in Germany from 1945–1949 were reported in the newsreels.

302   ALDGATE, Anthony. 'Covering civil war: the bombing of Guernica and the British cinema newsreels'. *The Media Reporter*, vol. 2, no. 4 (December 1978), p.22–3.

The *Gaumont-British News* issue no. 350, on Thursday 6 May 1937, was forthright in its condemnation of the destruction of Guernica, emphasising the destructive capacity of aerial bombing. However, Gaumont never went so far as *The Times* in accusing German planes of having been responsible for the bombing. Neither, like all the newsreel companies, did it ever explicitly accuse Franco of engaging any German planes to fight on his behalf. Yet the bombing did seem to have brought about a change of emphasis in the Gaumont coverage. Subsequent stories put more and more weight on aerial power and warfare. The other newsreels took up the theme and from then on regarded aerial warfare as a power to be reckoned with.

1979

303　ALDGATE, Anthony. *Cinema & history: British newsreels and the Spanish Civil War.* London: Scolar Press, 1979. xii, 234p.

A study of the organisation and structure of the British newsreels, examining their audiences, and analysing in detail their coverage of the Spanish War. Extensive filmography and bibliography.

304　BRIGGS, Asa. *The history of broadcasting in the United Kingdom. Vol. IV: Sound and Vision.* Oxford: OUP, 1979. xiv, 1082p.

Pages 588–99 discuss the setting up and early development of BBC television news. BBC *Television Newsreel* was first transmitted on 5 January 1948. (The last issue was televised on 2 July 1954). *News and Newsreel* began on 5 July 1954. The decision to introduce a regular Television *News Bulletin* was announced on 14 June 1955.

305　DOWNING, Taylor. *Palestine on film.* London: Council for the Advancement of Arab-British Understanding, 1979, 15p.

Begins with a survey of early photographic and cinematographic records of Palestine before moving on to discuss the Zionist documentaries of the 1930s and 1940s. The core of the author's argument is that 'the image created of the Palestinian Arab in documentary and news films up to 1948 was diametrically opposed to the image presented of the Zionist Jew'. Specific *British Movietone News* and *Pathé News* coverage is discussed as well as an issue of the American *March of Time*. Concludes that 'the Palestinians were never presented in the West as a society to be seen as equal to western civilized societies' and that 'the very positive and extensive representation of Zionism and its objectives in films and newsreels of the (1930s and 1940s) actually involved as part of its case, a denigration of the native Palestinian, a dismissal of his right to continue to live in the land of his forefathers and a stereotyping of the Arab as a backward, hostile and barbaric peasant'.

306　RAMSDEN, John. *Stanley Baldwin.* InterUniversity History Film Consortium, 1979. 21p. (Archive series no. 3).

Booklet which accompanies film of the same title. Introduces and discusses the newsreel extracts, in particular the context of the major speeches, used in the film with reference to Baldwin's speaking style.

307　KUEHL, Jerry. 'Cinema and History: British Newsreels and the Spanish Civil War, by Anthony Aldgate' (Review). *Sight & Sound*, vol. 48, no. 4 (Autumn 1979), p.265–6.

The long review raises the question of how newsreels can be both primary and secondary historical sources and the question of the motives and intentions of the newsreel makers.

1980

308　GRANT, Ian. *Cameramen at war.* Cambridge: Patrick Stephens (PSL), 1980. 192p.

A description of the work of the Army Film and Photographic Unit, of which the author was a member during the Second World War. Grant himself was mostly attached to armour formations and covered D-Day, the liberation of many cities in occupied Europe and the crossings of the Seine and the Rhine. He was the first man to film the horrors of Belsen concentration camp. He also describes the activities of his other Army cameraman colleagues in North Africa, with the Long-Range Desert Group, and in Italy. Many illustrations.

309 HOGENKAMP, Bert. '*Workers' newsreels in the 1920s and 30s*'. London: History Group of the Communist Party, 198–? 36p. (Our History series no. 68).

An international survey of Socialist newsreels. Section 6, p.11–14, discusses the history of *Workers' Topical News*. Section 9, p.16–21, discusses the 1933 British film 'What the newsreel does not show', which was intended to be the first newsreel of a series; the foundation of Kino; the four issues of *Workers' Newsreel*, and the Workers' Film & Photo League. A section on p.28–29 deals with the two issues of *People's Scrapbooks*, made by People's Newsreels.

310 THORPE, Frances and PRONAY, Nicholas and COULTASS, Clive. *British Official Films in the Second World War: a descriptive catalogue*. Oxford: Clio Press, 1980. x, 321p.

In his introduction, p.1–56, Nicholas Pronay discusses among other aspects, the debate at the beginning of the War on newsreels v. documentary films.

1981

311 HOLLINS, Timothy J. *The presentation of politics: the place of party publicity, broadcasting and film in British politics, 1918–39*. University of Leeds, PhD thesis (1981).

Chapter 9: 'The cinema newsreels and politics, 1929–1939', p.616–694, discusses the editorial policies of the newsreel companies and coverage of political events; details the relationship between the Foreign Office and the newsreel companies and the relationship that the Conservative Party had with British Movietone and Gaumont-British.

312 HOLLINS, Timothy. 'Postgraduate academic film research'. *Researcher's Guide to British Film & Television Collections*, edited by Elizabeth Oliver. London: British Universities Film Council, 1981. p.22–27.

Discusses, and gives advice on, how to research newsreel footage.

313 IMPERIAL WAR MUSEUM. *Welt im Film: a microfiche catalogue of the Imperial War Museum's holding of material from the Anglo-American newsreel screened in occupied Germany, 1945–1950*. London: IWM, 1981. 24 page booklet + 1 microfiche. (Microfiche Film Catalogue no. 1).

The catalogue, contained on a 42x fiche of 114 frames, gives film contents, release dates, running times, dates of shooting of unedited footage, etc. The booklet contains a six-page article by Roger B. N. Smither on the reel as well as a list of the issues and items missing from the IWM's collection: there are also instructions on how to consult the fiche.

314 MITCHELL, Leslie. *Leslie Mitchell reporting . . .* London: Hutchinson, 1981. 228p.

Autobiography of the radio and television commentator/interviewer. Includes sections covering his period as a newsreel commentator with *British Movietone News* during World War 2.

315 REEVES, Nicholas Anthony. *Official British film propaganda during the First World War*. University of London, PhD thesis (1981). 307p.

Chapter 3c, p.132–136 deals with the acquisition by the War Office Cinematograph Committee of a majority share-holding in the Topical Film Company and the setting up of the bi-weekly newsreel, *Topical Budget*, in its final phase to become known as *Pictorial News (Official)*.

316   HOLLINS, T. J. 'The Conservative Party and film propaganda between the wars'. *The English Historical Review*, vol. 96, no. 379 (April 1981), p.359–69.

A section of the article discusses the intricate relationship of the Conservative Party with the newsreel companies, in particular with British Movietone and Gaumont-British.

1982

317   PRONAY, Nicholas and SPRING, D. W. *Propaganda, politics and film, 1918–45*. London: Macmillan, 1982. ix, 302p.

Chapter 5, 'Baldwin and film', by J. A. Ramsden; Chapter 6, 'The workers' film movement in Britain, 1929–39' by Bert Hogenkamp; Chapter 8, 'The news media at war', by Nicholas Pronay; and Chapter 11, 'Films and the Home Front—the evaluation of their effectiveness by "Mass-Observation"', by Tom Harrisson, all deal in whole or in part with some aspect of the British newsreels.

Bombing of Nanking (1937). Chinese reinforcements moving into position. Note the German-style helmets. British Paramount News. *(still courtesy of the National Film Archive)*

Newsreel Organisations

THE NEWS AND SPECIALISED THEATRE ASSOCIATION OF GREAT BRITAIN AND NORTHERN IRELAND

This organisation was based at 31 Dover Street, Piccadilly, London W1. It was registered on 21st February 1939. The date of completion of the last audit was 13th February 1951. The existing records, comprising annual returns for the years 1939 to 1951, are held at the Public Record Office: reference no. FS 12/401.

The more important objects of the Association were:

1. To promote goodwill and understanding between the members, and secure legislation for the benefit of members and oppose measures detrimental to their mutual interests.
2. To ensure that the members shall maintain a high standard of service to the public; the minimum requirements to be determined by the Council from time to time.
3. To take steps to secure news films for presentation to the public which shall be free from censorship, political bias or propaganda, bearing in mind that in times of extreme national crisis, censorship from within or without the industry may be necessary in the interests of the State.
4. To encourage the production and circulation of short British and Foreign Films which have an Entertainment or Educational value, and to investigate and encourage the development of scientific research which is calculated to assist the members in the course of their business.

membership The returns give the following membership figures. (The *Kinematograph Year Book* totals which appeared for the years 1941–55 inclusive vary slightly and these figures are given in brackets.)—1939. 30: 1940. 36: 1941. 32 (36): 1942. 31 (35): 1943. 31 (32): 1944. 31 (32): 1945. 33 (32): 1946. 32 (31): 1947. 21 (31): 1948. 19 (20): 1949. 20 (21): 1950. 20 (21): 1951. (20): 1952. (20): 1953. (19): 1954. (18): 1955. (18). Approximately fifty news and specialised theatres in the United Kingdom were, however, according to *The Factual Film* (1947), represented by the Association. The 1941 *Kinematograph Year Book* listed among the members 9 theatres with the word 'news' in their titles: Topical News Cinema, Aberdeen; News Theatre, High Street, Birmingham; News Theatre, Peter Street, Bristol; News Theatre, City Road, Leeds; Victoria Station News Theatre, London; Waterloo Station News Theatre, London; World News Theatre, Praed Street, London W2; News Theatre, 16 Oxford Street, Manchester; and, The News House, Upper Parliament Street, Nottingham. The number of these news theatres remained constant more or less, though some of the names and locations changed.

theatres In 1943, according to the *Kinematograph Year Book* Capital and Provincial News Theatres Ltd, based at 100 Baker Street, London W1, owned the following news theatres: Embassy, Notting Hill Gate, London; Eros News Theatre, Shaftesbury Avenue, London; Victoria Station News Theatre, London; Vogue, Stoke Newington, London; Waterloo Station News Theatre, London; World's News Theatre, Praed Street, London; Tatler News Theatre, Liverpool; and the Classic, Southampton. By the end of the forties, according to the *British Film Yearbook 1949–50*, this company owned 21 cinemas. The existing records of Capital and Provincial News Theatres Ltd may be consulted at Companies House: reference 302,052. The company was dissolved on 31 December 1980.

In 1943 also, the Monseigneur News Theatre Circuit, based at 147 Wardour Street, London W1, operated these theatres: Time News Theatre, Baker Street Station, London; Monseigneur, Charing Cross, London: Monseigneur, Leicester Square, London: Monseigneur, Marble Arch, London; Monseigneur, Piccadilly, London; Monseigneur, Strand, London; Sphere News Theatre, Tottenham Court Road, London; and Monseigneur, Edinburgh (*Kinematograph Year Book*, 1943).

NEWSREEL ASSOCIATION OF GREAT BRITAIN AND IRELAND LTD

The objects of the Association, which was based at Film House, Wardour Street, London W1, were:

To promote and protect the interests, welfare and business of associates engaged in the production and distribution of cinematograph films depicting current events, known as Newsreels, and to bring about and maintain co-operation between them.

(*Kinematograph Year Book* 1942)

The existing records are in the care of:—Mr E. A. Candy, Director and General Manager, British Movietonews Ltd., North Orbital Road, Denham, near Uxbridge, Middlesex

Tel: 0895 833072

history
Founded in 1937. The Certificate of Incorporation is dated 31st October 1937 and the first meeting of the Council of the Association was held at 111 Wardour Street, London W1 on the 1st November 1937. Never formally dissolved the Association expired with the passing of the British newsreel era.

holdings
Five volumes of minutes, detailed and neatly typed with handwritten subject indexes, are extant.

Minutes of General Council Meetings
Minute Book no. 1: Minutes nos. 1–659, 1 November 1937–17 April 1941.
(Typical index entries: 'Rota subjects', 'Television—Television vans', 'Colonial newsreels'. Minute no. 144, pages 63–65, discusses 'National Film Library, BFI and preservation of newsreels'.)

Minute Book no. 2: Minutes 660–1491, 21 April 1941–15 December 1943
(Typical index entries: 'British Council', 'Royal Rota', 'British News', 'War Pictorial News'.)

Minute Book no. (?): Minutes 2657–4426, 28 October 1948–24 September 1953
(Typical index entries: 'Television' (many), 'Coronation' (many), 'Atomic Bomb material', ''Specialing' of football matches'.)

Minute Book no. (?): Minutes 4434–5490, 26 October 1953–20 May 1959
(Typical index entries: 'Newsreel theatres', 'Grand National', 'Monopolies & Restrictive Practices Commission', 'British Film Institute'.)

Minutes of Distribution Committee Meetings
Minute Book no. (?): Minutes 2435–5136, 10 November 1947–27 November 1956
(Typical index entries: 'Circulation of newsreels' (many), 'Dublin's first newsreel theatre', 'Sixteen millimetre newsreels and price schedule for' (many), 'Supplemental agreement' (many), 'Press statements by NRA'.)

access
Access to the records is restricted. Enquiries by *bona fide* researchers should be directed to Mr Candy.

The British newsreel companies: Staffing 1910–45.

Lisa Pontecorvo

Curiously there was never a move to identify newsreel cameramen as the 'stars' behind the newsreel story and so they remained anonymous, their pictures often memorable but their names unknown. This creates considerable problems for the film historian, if one wishes to work out how many cameramen a company had permanently on its staff, and how much cameramen moved between companies. The following list of British newsreel cameramen working from the pioneering days through to World War 2 is organised by company and alphabetically. It is largely a posthumous recognition of their work. Although it is not definitive, the list should serve as a useful basis to which names that have been unintentionally omitted could be added.

The information has been compiled by laboriously sifting through biographical entries in the earliest surviving *Kine Yearbooks* from 1920. Some of the entries refer back ten or twenty years to careers spent in the pioneering days of cinema in the early 1900s. Another useful source was the censored 'dope' sheets sent in by cameramen during World War 2 which have been preserved. Many of these men worked both before and after the War.

Certain facts emerge from the list. Broadly speaking the newsreel companies had relatively small permanent staffs of 6–10 cameramen. There does not seem to have been a rapid turnover rate nor much movement between companies. There seem to have been newsreel families such as the Gemmells, the Jeapes, the Nobles, the Samuelsons, and the Wyands. Most newsreel cameramen were specialised and did not work in feature film production with the exception of Stanley Mumford (*Empire News Bulletin* and Universal) and H. W. Bishop of Gaumont.

In 1977 I interviewed several British newsreel cameramen whose memories seem to corroborate the evidence of the lists. H. W. Bishop confirmed that Gaumont Graphic had had six London-based staff cameramen and another ten in the provinces, when as technical manager in 1926 he was the person responsible for deploying them. The Glasgow, Manchester, Cardiff and Liverpool cameramen of Gaumont even had a small laboratory on hand to process and print their stories. The other six were based in Bristol, Birmingham, Leeds, Edinburgh, Dublin and Belfast. As they added a few more cameramen and sound engineers to the staff, with the coming of sound in about 1932, Bishop had eight sound crews (i.e. cameramen and recordists) to deploy round the country from London. For big events the newsreel companies increased their complement of cameramen, for example, thirty-four were needed for the Grand National.

Empire News Bulletin, which later became *Universal Talking News*, had six London staff cameramen and three based in Manchester, Scotland and Wales according to Stanley Mumford, who was with the *Bulletin* in the late 1920s. Leslie Murray was a member of the London office of Movietone when it was first set up, and he confirmed that there were 4 cameramen. Norman Roper stated that British Pathé had 4–6 London-based cameramen in the thirties.

In the 1920s the Editor was less of a public figure than in the 1930s. With the coming of sound commentaries, Movietone's editor Gerald Sanger shared the editing with Ivan Scott and specialised commentators. But this was unusual in that British Paramount had only one editor, Tom Cummins, as did Gaumont with Louis Behr, Pathé with Tom Scales, and Universal with Cecil Snape. The mid-thirties saw the rise of the professional commentator in the newsreels. Paramount used two unidentified voices to read the commentary; Universal, *Gaumont-British News* and *Pathé Gazette* believed in a single, identified commentator cast in a sort of star part. *British Movietone News* on the other hand, appointed a number of well-known authorities as commentators who were identified on the newsreel: R. Lyle and Sir Malcolm Campbell for racing commentaries: H. B. T. Wakeham, a football forward, to do sport; Eric Dunstan and Alan Howland, both former BBC announcers, and Leslie Mitchell and Ivan Scott, who was also the news editor. Although they were authorities on their subjects they were not apparently allowed to script their own commentaries. Only E. V. H. Emmett, the commentator for *Gaumont-British News*, was allowed to control the cutting of the sound film so that his own scripted commentary matched the picture. *June 1983*

British Newsreel Company Staff up to and including World War 2

This list, which does not claim to be exhaustive, is in two parts. The first arrangement is by company up to 1939 and indicates staff whose careers continued into World War 2. It does not include World War 2 staff whose careers started after 1939. The second list is alphabetical and includes all those known to be working up to 1945. Dates cover the beginning and not necessarily the end of the careers up to 1945.

1.   COMPANY LIST (Pre-World War 2)

TOPICAL BUDGET

T. W. Cotton	pre 1921	(moved to Pathé)
Walter Evan Davies	1918–19	War Office Topical Budget
J. G. Gemmell	May 1919–20	
R. Harris	c.1919–pre 1931	when moved to Movietone
Charles F. T. Heath	1921–28	
John Bunney Hutchins	1921–28	
Harold J. Jeapes	1920–c.1922	
Harold G. Jones	1928–30	
George Plowman	1934	
John A. Parry	1915–23	
P. Tobin	1930–38	
Fred L. Wilson	1921–25	
George Woods Taylor	1911–14	Editor, and first slow motion news film, official film landing BEF
Frank Danvers Yates	1923–24	

PATHE

F. A. Bassill	1922–38	
Jack Cotter	pre 1934 for many years	WACA Yearsley-Snd Recordist 1933–36
G. W. Cotton	1921–22	
Sidney Easton	1920s	
Arthur Farmer	?1924, 1934–44 WW2	
J. G. Gemmell	April 1912–WW1 June 1920–WW2	
Ken Gordon	?1921–WW2	
Charles F. T. Heath	c.1914	
James S. Hodgson	?pre WW1	
Harold G. Jones	1934–35	
Arthur W. Kingston	1919–26	
J. Gordon Lewis	1921–26	Pathé News in America, Pathé Gazette and Pathé News in Ireland
Charles R. Martin	1934–WW2	
Joe Noble	pre 1928	
G. W. Pockwell	1921–26?	
Gaston Quiribet	1905–11	(Pathé Frères)
M. Redknapp	1933–39	
I. Roseman	c.1910–12; 1933	(Filmed 1st British dirigible)
Henry Armitage Sanders	1910–36	1st English operator for PG; Editor 1919–34
Thomas F. Scales	1915–30	

Harry Starner	1913–36	
James Taylor I	1910–14	(Dark room Pathé Frères)
Leslie Wyand	1912–15; 1919–31	British Correspondent for Pathé News in USA
Frank Danvers Yates	1916–21	British correspondent for Pathé News in USA
W. J. Gell		newsreel association representative 1939
Norman Roper	1948–70	Chief cutter; make-up editor; Deputy Editor; Editor; General Manager.

GAUMONT

Silent cameramen

A. Albert Any	1920–60	Any Gaumont Graphic and GBN titles/special effects
H. W. Bishop	1910–36	(darkroom)
	1936	technical photographic manager
	1910–20	cameraman
W. Boel	1910–?	
Oscar F. Bovill	1908–1909	
John Y. Brown	1905–?1911	
Hugh T. Callender	1919–21	
William C. Carrington	1905	(Darkroom) and then camera – 1914
Walter Evan Davies	1912–14	(from start of news film)
Basil Emmott	1921–26	
Charles F. T. Heath	post 1919–21	
James S. Hodgson	1916	
John Bunney Hutchins	1908–?1920s	
Leslie Murray	1928–29	
Arthur A. Richardson	1912–26	
Jack H. Ross	1927–36	
James Taylor	?1920–30	
Leslie Wyand	1910–11	(Liverpool Office) Hearst Rep with Gaumont Snd News 1934–38

Sound cameramen

A. Berger	1936	
H. Bromige	1933–39	Gaumont Sound News
	1938–39	news and contact manager
P. Cannon	1933–47	
A. R. Edmonds	1933–WW2	
? M. Ford	1936	GB Screen Services
G. Golding	1933–39	
Edward H. Hawkins	1939–42	
?Gunther Krampf	1931–36	1st cameraman Gaumont-British News Lighting Cameraman
H. Morley	1933–42	
E. Owen	1933–37	

Sound recordists

H. Abbott	1933–39	Sound recordist and chief engineer
A. Birch	1939	Chief recordist
W. Burningham	1933–36	Sound recordist
H. Fraser	1938	recorder
H. Fuller	1933–34	recordist
W. Hooker	1933–39	sound recordist
K. Maskell	1933–35	sound recordist

A. Prentice	1938–39	recorder
C. Pryke	1934–35	sound recordist
R. Read	1933–37	sound recordist
E. Runkell	1938–39	recorder
D. Tate	1933–35	sound recordist

Commentators

| Jack Anderson | 1933–35 | |
| E. V. H. Emmett | 1936–39 | Film Editor and commentator from 1930 |

Editors

L. F. Behr	1933–37	Editorial Manager Gaumont Snd News and Sound Mirror
Jeffrey Bernerd	1939	Representative on Newsreel Association of Great Britain
Andrew Buchanan	1934–37	Gaumont Sound Mirror Editor
R. Drew	1922–29	Cutter
	1929–59	Editor GBN Sound
W. C. Gimber	1933–37	Associate Editor GBN
R. S. Howard	1933–39	Editor Gaumont Sound News
L. Castleton-Knight	1939–48	Producer GBN
H. R. Parsons	1933–37	Associate Editor GBN
W. Rowe	1938–39	Assistant Editor GBN
Charles Saunders	1937–38	Editorial cutter

MOVIETONE

Cameramen

Jack Cotter	1934–36	Chief cameraman
	1936–38	Production Manager with company until 1948
R. Harris	1931–WW2	
Leslie Murray	1929–38	
George Plowman	1934–35	
Alfred A. Tunwell	1929–WW2	
Paul Wyand	1931–WW2	

Commentator

| Leslie Mitchell | 1938–46 | |

Sound

| Patrick Wyand | 1934–74 | |

Editors

H. O. K. Ayling	1933–34	News Editor
Sir Malcolm Campbell	1934–39	Editor
Sir Gordon Craig	1936–39	Director and General Manager
L. L. Landau	1935	Asst. Editor Movietone
Norman Roper	1948–70	Chief Newsreel Editor
G. F. Sanger	1929–54	Director Producer
B. B. Saveall	1934–37	News editor Movietone
Thomas F. Scales	1938	Asst. Editor Movietone
	1928–34	Production Manager
Ivan Scott	1938–39	News Editor

Graphics

Eunice Wyand

PARAMOUNT

Cameramen

Fred Bayliss	1936–WW2	
Arthur Farmer	WW2	
Maurice Ford	1937–38–WW2	
J. Gemmell	1936	
Fred Wilson	1930–33	

Editors

Oswald Brooks	1933–35	Executive assistant
G. T. Cummins	1933–39	Assistant then Editor, General Editor, Paramount.
W. Harcourt	1932–36	Make-up Editor Paramount Sound News 1935–36, Cutter 1932–34
James W. Mellor	1921–WW2	Chief cutter and make-up editor Paramount
Norman Roper	1931–48	Shipping, News, Library, cutting room
John Slee	1933–34	News Editor Paramount

Technical staff

L. W. Green	1937–39	Assistant Technical Supervisor
K. F. Hanson	1933–37	Technical supervisor

UNIVERSAL

Cameramen

John Bunney Hutchins	1934–?1938	
Harold J. Jeapes	1936–38	Universal (1922–35 Empire News Bulletin)
Stanley J. Mumford	1923–30	(British Pictorial)
Ronnie Noble	1939–WW2	
Fred L. Wilson	?1934–1938–WW2	(1926 Empire News Bulletin)

Editors

S. F. Ditcham	1939	Representative on Newsreel Association of Great Britain
Clifford W. Jeapes	1934–39	Studio director and director/producer Universal News to 1948
William C. Jeapes	1934–39	Universal News and Empire News Bulletin Managing Director
B. B. Saveall	1939	Universal Studio Director
Cecil R. Snape	1934–37	Editor Universal News
Leslie Murray	1944	Production Manager Universal
	1947	Editor

BRITISH SCREEN NEWS

John Bunney Hutchins	1929–33	Chief Cameraman
James S. Hodgson		Editor and Manager British Screen News

2. ALPHABETICAL LISTING

Newsreel Cameramen

Terry Ashwood	WW2	Pathé
H. E. Ashwood	WW2	Pathé
A. E. Aubury	1939–WW2	Gaumont-British
George Arthur Barrett	1926	RNAS in World War 1
Jack Barnett	WW2	Movietone
? Barne	WW2	Gaumont-British News
Eric Barrow	WW2	Universal
Frank A. Bassill	1922–WW2	Warwick 1908, Pathé Gazette 1930s
A. Berger	1936	Gaumont-British News
Fred W. Bayliss	1936–WW2	British Paramount
M. J. Benson	1921–29	WW1 and earlier
H. W. Bishop	1910–39	Gaumont and Production Manager GBN 1945
Bob Blair	1944	Pathé
A. H. Bloomfield	1921–26	B & C and Walter West
Sydney Blythe	1910–26	Jury, New Era et alia Will Barker, Samuelsons Twickenham
S. R. G. Bonnett	1929–WW2	Everest Expedition and WW2— Stoll Gaumont
Bonney Powell	1940	?
W. Bool	1910–26	Gaumont, Williamsons, Barkers
Oscar F. Bovill	1908–36	Gaumont, Barkers, London Underground
F. O. Bovill	WW2	Pathé
John Y. Brown	1905–25	Gaumont, Williamsons
H. Bromige	1933–39	Gaumont Sound News, Snd Mirror & 1938–39 News and Contact Manager
? Burnie	WW2	
Jack Burnett (USA)	WW2	GBN-BMN
Hugh T. Callender	1919–21	Gaumont
William G. Carrington	1905–38	Gaumont, Vickers
A. E. 'Ted' Candy	1940–42	Gaumont-British News
P. E. Cannon	1933–47	Gaumont-British
L. H. Cave-Chinn	WW2	British Paramount News
Jack Christian	1908–24	Charles Urban
D. P. Cooper	1908–26	Cricks and Martin, Broadwest, Homeland, Stoll
T. W. Cotton	1921–22	Pathé Gazette after Topical Budget
Jack Cotter	1930–48	Pathé, British Movietone News
Walter Evan Davies	1912–24	Gaumont, Warwick Chronicle, Williamson, War Office, Topical
A. R. Edmonds	WW1–1933–WW2	Gaumont-British – filmed WW1
Sydney Easton	1928–38	Hepworth, Pathé
Basil Emmott	1921–26	Gaumont + 1st flight to SA—later Stoll (feature)
James Ewins	WW2	Gaumont-British News
Arthur W. Farmer	1921–WW2	Paramount and Pathé
Norman Fisher	WW2–1976	Movietone 1976
Claude H. Friese-Greene	1905–35	Eclair Jnl, BFC, Own Co.
Maurice Ford	1937–WW2	British Lion, London Fox, Paramount Sound News
Jim Gemmell	WW2	British Paramount News
Jock G. Gemmell	1910–WW2	Warwick, Topical Budget, Pathé Gazette
E. P. Genock	WW2	British Paramount News

G. Golding	1933–39	GBN
Kenneth R. L. G. Gordon	1912–WW2	World War 1 and Pathé
Edward T. Grant	1912–24	
Edward H. Hawkins	1911–38	Kinetos, Paramount, Gaumont-British News
W. Harcourt	1932–36	Cutter 1932–34
		Paramount Make-up Editor 1934–36
J. C. Harding	WW2–1948	Paramount
Douglas H. J. Hardy	WW2	Paramount
J. Harris	1916–25	Gaumont
Richard Harris	1908–WW2	Warwick Chronicle, RFC, Topical Budget, Movietone 1931
Harvey Harrison	1896–1935	Worked with Dr Gaveaux, Friese-Greene, Colin Bennett, Barkers, Gaumont
Ben R. Hart	WW2	British Paramount News
E. H. Hawkins	1939–WW2	Gaumont-British News, Paramount
Charles F. T. Heath	1913–38	B & C Gaumont, Topical, Pathé
John Heddon	WW2	Pathé
? Higgins	WW2	Paramount
James S. Hodgson	1916–36	Pathé, Gaumont, March of Time and Major Post Screen News 1929
James Humphries	1933–37	Gaumont-British News
John Bunney Hutchins	1908–38	Topical, Gaumont, British Screen News, Universal
Harold J. Jeapes	1899–1938	Warwick, Director Topical, Universal, ENB 1922–35
Harold G. Jones	1906–35	Topical Budget, Pathé Gazette
Gunther Krampf	c.1935	1st cameraman Gaumont-British
Arthur Kingston	1907–26	Warwick, Pathé
F. W. Lachland	WW2	Gaumont-British
Emile Louis Lauste	1894–1926	USA, and the Biograph, Welsh Pearson
J. Gordon Lewis	1911–26	Pathé News
Alan Lawson	1934	Chief cameraman Baird TV
Harold Mease Lomas	1900–26	Technical Manager Minerva Film
Jack Lieb	WW2	Pathé
W. M. Macgregor	WW2	British Paramount News
Frank McLachlan	WW2	Gaumont-British News
J. C. Bee Mason	1914–26	WW1 Kinematographer, Arctic Exped.
Charles R. Martin	1934–WW2	Pathé
Archak Masraff	1940	Hearst for GBN
Eric Mayell	WW2	Movietone
Arthur Meriless	WW2	Paramount
H. J. Morley	1933–WW2	Gaumount-British
Stanley J. Mumford	1906–30	Williamson, British Pictorial Prods. Oldest survivor filmed 1913 suffragette Derby and Chaplin's first film
Leslie Murray	1928–38	Gaumont Graphic, British Movietone, Editor Universal 1947
Joe Noble	1928–29	Pathé
Ronnie Noble	1939–WW2	British Pictorial, Universal
George B. Oswald	WW2	Universal
E. Owen	1933–37	Gaumont-British News
George Plowman	1934–38	Topical Budget, British Movietone
John H. Parry	1915–23	Topical
G. W. Pockwell	1921–35	Pathé US Companies
J. Preston Criff	pre 1906–26	Urbanora, Kineto
? Primavera	WW2	Movietone

? Prosser	WW2	Movietone
Frank 'Taxi' Purnell	WW2	Universal
Gaston Quiribet	1905–26	Pathé Frères, Hepworth
Jack L. Ramsden	WW2	Paramount, Pathé, Movietone
Ronald L. Read	WW2	British Paramount News
M. Redknapp	1933–39	Pathé
Arthur A. Richardson	1912–36	Gaumont
I. Roseman	1904–38	Barkers, Warwick, Pathé
Jack H. Ross	1909–38	War cameraman South Africa, British Army WW1, Spanish Government 1936, Gaumont
John Salter	1895–1927	Camera expert and inventor. Worked with Friese-Greene
David Samuelson	1940	BMN
Sidney Samuelson	1940	
Henry Armitage Sanders	1908–36	Pathé Gazette—became Editor PG
Charles Saunders	1937–38	Gaumont-British editorial cutter
Thomas F. Scales	1905–38	Pathé Gazette and British Movietone (Editor BMN)
Arthur Smith	1896–1925	Walturdaw, McDowells Commercial Film
Gerard Somers	WW2	Pathé Gazette
Harry Starner	1913–38	Pathé Gazette
Albert Stockwell	1930s	Paramount
Ian Struthers	WW2 1942–47	Gaumont-British News and Paramount
Neil Sullivan	WW2	Pathé
Edward Tassie	WW2	Universal
James Taylor	1910–30	Pathé Frères, Eclair, Cines Gaumont
John Taylor	WW2	Universal
Graham Thompson	WW2	Movietone
Theodore R. Thumwood	1905–29	Clarendon, Martin, Master Film
P. Tobin	1918–38	Fox, British Instructional, Topical Budget
Alec Tozer	WW2	Movietone
H. Turner	1939–WW2	Gaumont-British Librarian 1939
P. J. Turner	WW2	Gaumont-British News
Alfred A. Tunwell	1911–38, WW2	Samuelson, British Lion, Movietone 1929
? Wilquin	WW2	Paramount
A. T. Willis	WW2	Gaumont-British
Fred L. Wilson	1911–WW2	Kineto, Topical Budget, Empire News, Paramount, Universal, Pathé
Howard Winner	WW2	Pathé
R. Colwyn Wood	WW2	Universal
George Woods Taylor	1911–38	Topical Film, Kinechrome
H. S. 'Newsreel' Wong	WW2	Gaumont-British, Fox
E. J. H. Wright	1937–WW2	Paramount-Deputy Editor Cummins
Leslie Wyand	1910–38	Gaumont Graphic, Pathé Gazette, Gaumont Sound News, Hearst rep.
Paul Wyand	1931–WW2	Movietone
Frank Danvers Yates	1911–25	Barkers, Cherry Kearton, Pathé News and Fox (USA)

Commentators

David Abercrombie	WW2	War Pictorial News
John Anderson	1933–35	Gaumont-British News
Patrick Acquilar	1946	World Pictorial News
Eric Dunstan	1930s	BMN

E. V. Emmett	1936–39	Gaumont-British News (Cutter from 1930) Stayed till 1944
Frank Hurley	WW2	War Pictorial News
Rex Keating	WW2	War Pictorial News
C. R. Martin	WW2	War Pictorial News
Robert Noble	WW2	War Pictorial News
Pat O'Malley	WW2	War Pictorial News
Leslie Mitchell	WW2	War Pictorial News
Rory Patouillet	WW2	War Pictorial News
John Redway	WW2	War Pictorial News
Vera Clive Smith	WW2	War Pictorial News
Ivan Scott	WW2–1930s	BMN
John Stag	1936	Pathé, BMN
F. H. G. Taylor	WW2	War Pictorial News
Bob Danvers Walker	1940	BMN, Pathé

Non-Cameramen

H. Abbott	1933–39	Gaumont-British sound recordist, later chief recording engineer
Edgar Anstey	1938	Director March of Time
H. O. K. Ayling	1933–34	News Editor Movietone
L. F. Behr	1933–37	Editorial Manager Gaumont Sound News and Sound Mirror
Jeffrey Bernerd	1939	Gaumont-British representative Newsreel Assoc. of GB
A. Birch	1939	Gaumont-British News Chief recordist
E. Oswald Brooks	1933–35	Executive Assistant Paramount
Alex Braid	1914	Editor Gaumont Graphic
D. W. Brunaugh	1938	Director March of Time
Andrew Buchanan	1934–37	Gaumont Sound Mirror Magazine editor
W. Burningham	1933–36	Sound recordist Gaumont-British News
Sir Malcolm Campbell	1934–39	Editor British Movietone
Sir Gordon Craig	1936–39	British Movietone, Director and General Manager
G. T. Cummins	1933–39	Assistant and then Editor and General Manager Paramount
G. W. Dawson	1938	Director March of Time
S. F. Ditcham	1939	Representative for Universal on Newsreel Assoc. of GB
R. Drew	1929–59	Cutter Gaumont-British News, Editor Sound News 1929–59
H. Fraser	1938	Recorder Gaumont-British News
H. Fuller	1933–34	Sound Recordist Gaumont-British News
W. J. Gell	1939	Pathé Representative of Newsreel Association of GB
Leslie Gentle	?	BMN – Sound
W. C. Gimber	1933–37	Associate Editor Gaumont-British News
L. W. Green	1937–39	Assistant Technical Supervisor Paramount
Martin Gray	WW2	BMN
A. Grosvenor	1939	Gaumont-British News Librarian
Ralph Hansbury	1938	Director March of Time
K. F. Hanson	1933–37	Technical Supervisor Paramount
W. Hooker	1933–39	Sound Recordist Gaumont-British News
R. S. Howard	1933–39	Editor Gaumont Sound News and Sound Mirror

Clifford W. Jeapes	1934–39	Universal Studio direction
William C. Jeapes	1934–39	Universal News and Empire News Bulletin Managing Director
L. Castleton-Knight	1939–48	Producer Gaumont-British News
Nevil Kearney	1939	Secretary of Newsreel Association of GB
L. L. Landau	1935	Assistant Editor Movietone
Roy E. Larson	1938	Chairman March of Time London Office
E. Law	1936–39	Assistant and then Technical Supervisor Paramount
W. S. Macpherson	1933	Pathétone Studios art direction
K. Maskell	1933–35	Sound Recordist Gaumont-British News
James W. Mellor	1922–33–WW2	Chief cutter and make-up Editor Paramount
George Newberry	1935–39	Pathétone Studios sound recordist
H. R. Parsons	1933–?37	Associate Editor Gaumont-British News
A. Prentice	1938–39	Recorder Gaumont-British News
C. Pryke	1934–35	Gaumont-British News Sound Recordist
R. Read	1933–37	Gaumont-British News Sound Recordist
Richard D. Rochemont	1938	Managing Director March of Time London
Norman Roper	1938–76	Paramount, Pathé, Movietone Editor
W. Rowe	1938–39	Assistant Editor (cutter) Gaumont-British News
E. Runkel	1938–39	Recorder Gaumont-British News
G. F. Sanger	1929–54	Director and Producer Movietone
B. B. Saveall	1934–39	News Editor Movietone, Universal Studio Director 1939
Dennis F. Scanlon	1938	March of Time Sound
Ivan Scott	1938–39	News Editor Movietone
John Slee	1933–34	News Editor Paramount
Cecil R. Snape	1934–37	Editor Universal News
Charles L. Stillman	1938	Director March of Time
D. Tate	1933–35	Gaumont-British News Sound Recordist
F. Watts	1933–39	Pathétone Studios Studio Manager
Patrick Wyand	1934–74	BMN Sound
J. R. Wood Jnr.	1938	Director March of Time
W.A.C.A. Yearsley	1933–36	Pathétone Studios Sound Recordist

Arrest of suffragette outside Buckingham Palace. Pathé newsreel 1914. Catalogue no. N.757. (still courtesy of National Film Archive)

Newsreel Libraries and Archives

BRITISH MOVIETONE FILM LIBRARY

North Orbital Road, Denham, Uxbridge, Middlesex

Tel: 0895-832323

contact   Miss Pat Holder, Film Librarian

history   In addition to *British Movietone News* (1929–29 April 1979), the Library holds the Henderson Film Library (1895/6–World War 1), the Pinewood Feature Film Stock Shot Library and the *Look at Life* Series Stock Shot Library (35mm, Eastmancolour).

holdings   There is no accurate figure but the total footage is estimated to be around 80 million, rising possibly to 100 million feet of 35mm film. This figure includes the Pinewood stock shot material. Only 20 years of the newsreel material is on nitrate stock, 25 years is on safety stock. As Movietone no longer produces newsreels, the main part of the library staff's work is on information retrieval.

components   These components are held for newsreel material: a) combined lavender print (i.e. a black & white fine grain master positive print for duping purposes), b) cut negative, and c) show copy. Other earlier material is on negative or positive stock depending on which component was received by the Library.

storage   The material is stored in 33 vaults adjacent to the Library. The vaults were built in 1961 to the specification of the Home Office and were approved by the factory inspectors. In addition, there are open space free standing racks and moving racks on runners.

cataloguing   *The Card Catalogue of Newsreel Material*—contains the main entry index cards and the cross index cards. *The 'Look at Life' Card Index; Pinewood Feature Film Stock Shot Library Record Books*—these are in various volumes in which the stock shots are illustrated as well as being described. *The Screen Record Book*—this is in various volumes. It records every piece of film which comes into Movietone, regardless of what happens to it afterwards. Runs in date order. Starts in 1934–5, no entries then until 1937 from when there are entries to date. Gives title, file number, length of material, usually what has happened to the material subsequent to its arrival at the Library (e.g. J = junked, H = hold, etc). *General Release Stockbook*—this records what goes into the individual newsreels and what the Library has in the way of negatives.

documentation Movietone News issue sheets, 9 June 1929–29 April 1979. Commentary sheets (separate for the years 1929–46; with issue sheets from 1946/7–1979. Printed texts of speeches are not available).

junking   Only off-cuts from new material are junked nowadays. Material is junked where the physical quality of the stock is bad or where the content is 'not of interest'.

access   Researchers are encouraged to visit the Library by appointment and do their own research. There is no charge for using the catalogue. The only impediment here is the number of people that can work at the catalogue at any one time. If the library staff do research for anyone a service fee may be charged. The moment film is used, for viewing purposes or otherwise, there is a charge. A sheet listing the current purchase charges is available from the Library. Because the Library needs to make a profit, discounts for copying film are not given to educational bodies.

IMPERIAL WAR MUSEUM

Lambeth Road, London SE1 6HZ

Tel: 01-735-8922 Ext. 251

contact   Paul Sargent, Production Information Officer

history   The collection was founded in 1919 when copies of the official films which had been made in Britain during the First World War were handed over to the Museum (itself founded in 1917) for preservation. From the Second World War the Museum was able to take over all the unedited film shot by the service film units as well as many documentary and official films and significant collections of foreign material. The archive is not, however, limited to the World Wars: the Museum's terms of reference include all aspects of military operations involving Britain and the Commonwealth since August 1914. Neither is film acquired solely through Government deposit—coverage of many events, including more recent conflicts, is acquired by gift, purchase or exchange from individuals, commercial companies and other archives.

holdings   The current estimate of the total size of the collection is 60 million feet representing probably some 35,000 separate units (the collection cannot, because of the preponderance of unedited film, be described in terms of titles). Practically all of this film is non-fiction and almost half of it is unedited record footage, much of which is supported by 'dope-sheets', the cameraman's records compiled at the time of shooting. The principal unedited holdings relate to the three British armed services in the Second World War to British and German technological developments and to Britain's railways during the Second World War. Unedited camera rushes shot by British newsreel cameramen (Gaumont-British, Movietone, Paramount, Pathé and Universal) on the war fronts between 1939–45 are also held.

Newsreels in fact form a significant and growing sub-collection.

The Museum holds complete runs of two British official Second World War newsreels, *War Pictorial News* and *Warwork News*, 120 issues of an official US newsreel *United News* released between 1943 and 1945, as well as extensive collections of German and Soviet newsreels also from the Second World War period. In addition there are 127 issues of an Indian official newsreel *Indian News Parade* released between late 1943 and 26 April 1946 and 13 issues of *Indian Movietone News* all released between February and August 1943. A few Japanese newsreels are also held.

The immediate post-war period is covered by the series *Welt Im Film* which was shown in the British and American zones of Germany from 1945–50.

The holdings of British commercial newsreels for the war years were until recently far less comprehensive. For the most part there were only scattered individual issues from the output of all the major companies, the Movietone holdings being the exception since a more or less continuous run existed for the years 1942–45.

A few years ago, however, it was agreed that the Museum and the National Film Archive, should share the preservation of the Visnews nitrate collection (Gaumont Graphic, Gaumont-British, Paramount and Universal); the Museum taking responsibility for the years 1914–18 and 1939–45. Most of the silent Gaumont Graphic material for the First World War, most of the Gaumont-British issues for the Second World War and much of the Paramount News Library material for the war period is now held, but some material remains to be transferred from the NFA. Part of the collection has already been copied onto safety stock and some viewing prints are available.

The Museum and the NFA are also co-operating with the Thorn-EMI-Pathé Library on a major preservation programme which aims to transfer their nitrate newsreel holdings to safety stock. Work has begun on the 1914–18 period and it is hoped to complete the copying of this part of the Pathé collection within three to four years. Copying of the 1939–45 Pathé Gazettes will then begin.

Similarly the Museum has begun copying some of the Movietone newsreels for the Second World War, concentrating naturally on those issues that are not already held.

Other significant sub-collections include First and Second World War official films including many produced under the auspices of the Ministry of Information, a growing collection of television material, including unedited interview material filmed for series such as 'The Great War', 'The World at War', 'Palestine', and 'The Troubles', and some very interesting collections of amateur film.

components   The Museum, for preference, holds each unit of film in at least three forms—fine grain print, negative and viewing print. Naturally, by no means all material is acquired in this form and many films ar held only as unique copies. About two thirds of the collection is on nitrate stock; the Museum's preservation programme is gradually copying nitrate material onto safety stock and, as funds permit, producing the extra copies necessary to 'open up' the collection. Less than ten per cent of the collection is colour material; at the moment, very little videotape is held but the Museum attempts to acquire preservation copies on broadcast standard format and make material available for viewing on video cassette.

storage   Nitrate film is stored in purpose-built vaults at Hayes, Middlesex. Acetate film is now stored in specially converted stores with controlled temperature and relative humidity at the Museum's outstation at Duxford Airfield. Theatre copies of a few films are kept permanently at the Museum's main building.

cataloguing   The Museum has two generations of documentation. First, catalogues and indexes produced by the original holder of the material and acquired with the film (these are generally subject indexes to each separate 'series' of film—e.g., the Army Film Unit's coverage of the campaign in North-West Europe, 1944–45). Second, a programme of re-cataloguing and indexing the entire collection, which is being carried out by the Museum's Department of Information Retrieval. Begun in manual form, the latter is now computerised; from 1975, the Museum used its own computer package APPARAT, but since 1982 has switched film cataloguing to the Museum Documentation Association's package GOS, which was already in use for the Museum's other collections. Some 6,000 films have so far been entered on the computer catalogue, including the Museum's holdings of *Movietone*, *Warwork News* and *Welt Im Film* newsreel materials.

The Museum has to date published only one catalogue in microfiche form (though bound in an explanatory booklet). It describes the collection of *Welt Im Film* the newsreel shown in the British and US zones of Germany, 1945–50. Also published is a guide to the 94 films (including 31 newsreels) available to universities through the Museum's loan scheme.

documentation   Dope sheets are held for British Army and RAF film unit material as well as for most of the unedited camera rushes shot by British newsreel cameramen on the war fronts; shot lists for this material and for some other collections are also available.

Scripts are held for a number of the official newsreels series, including *War Pictorial News*, *Indian News Parade* and the US newsreel *United News*. Commentary translations are held for the Russian newsreel collection and there are also translations for a number of the German films although most of the German newsreels are documented only by shot lists.

Files relating to the transfer of film and photographic material to the Museum from the First World War Ministry of Information and files including scripts and correspondence relating to some Second World War Ministry of Information films are also held.

The Museum's collection of photographs comprehensively supplements the collection of official record film for both World Wars and the Museum's library also has a small section of books on film, propaganda etc.

junking The Museum does not intentionally destroy any material. Occasionally, nitrate material is found on acquisition to have deteriorated beyond redemption, but otherwise no material is destroyed uncopied.

access It is the Museum's policy to help both academic and commercial researchers. All material is in principle available for viewing at the Museum although there are practical problems when a film is held as a unique copy. It must also be stressed that where British commercial newsreel material is involved film and television researchers should always apply directly to the newsreel libraries holding copyright in the material; academics, students or private individuals wishing to view newsreels strictly for research purposes are of course welcome to view at the Museum wherever viewing prints are available.

A small charge is made for prolonged private or academic research; details of charges, reproduction fees and commercial rates are available on request.

NATIONAL FILM ARCHIVE

81 Dean Street, London W1V 6AA

Tel: 01-437 4355

contact Roger Holman, Chief Cataloguer
Elaine Burrows, Viewings Supervisor
Christine Kirby, Production Librarian

history The National Film Archive began its existence in May 1935, in fulfilment of one of the ten aims of the British Film Institute, namely 'to maintain a national repository of films of permanent value'. In the fifties, the Archive began systematically to select and acquire television programmes as well as films for preservation, and in 1961 the BFI's brief was officially extended to include television. The Archive's main purpose is to select, acquire, preserve, document and make permanently available for research and study a national collection of films and television programmes of all kinds exhibited or transmitted in the UK, from any source and of any nationality, which have lasting value as works of art, examples of cinema and television history, historical or scientific records, portraiture, or records of contemporary life and behaviour.

holdings At April 1983 the total number of films in the Archive stood at over 75,000 titles, comprising feature and fiction films, shorts, documentaries, newsreels, amateur films and television programmes, ranging in period from 1895 to the present day.

Current rate of acquisition runs at about 2,000 items a year, including videotapes.

components Ideally an original negative or fine grain print is held as the master preservation copy, accompanied by a working negative and a viewing print. This ideal is rarely achieved but is the Archive's ultimate aim. Videotape is normally preserved on broadcast-standard format and made available for viewing in videocassette form.

storage All material is housed and cared for at the Archive's three out-of-London sites. Safety film (narrow gauges and most 35mm films made after 1951) and videotapes are kept in air-conditioned stores at Ernest Lindgren House, Berkhamsted. Nitrate film (most 35mm films made before 1951), because it is inflammable and subject to inevitable and irreversible chemical deterioration, is stored in 216 specially constructed vaults at a remote site at Gaydon, Warwickshire. Aston Clinton, which was until recently the main depository for nitrate film, remains the Archive's technical centre, where the principal work of restoration and conservation is performed, and serves also as a secondary store for safety film.

cataloguing

Preliminary Title List (Kalamazoo)—this is the most important index in the sense that it lists all of the NFA's holdings. In these large binders fiction films, newsfilm, documentaries and TV programmes are listed alphabetically by title. The feature and documentary record is in four parts, providing: 1) the alphabetical title list, 2) the index of directors, 3) country and date index, and 4) production company index. The newsfilm record is in two parts providing a) the alphabetical title list and b) the chronological index. *Main entry cards* (i.e. shotlists)—items which have been viewed and fully catalogued are recorded on main entry cards. They are listed by title or, in the case of newsfilm, by date. *Main subject index*—classified by UDC.

Published catalogues available: *Catalogue. Part 1. Silent Newsfilms 1895–1933*; *Catalogue. Part 3. Silent Fiction Films, 1895–1930*; *Catalogue of Viewing Copies (1971)*; *Catalogue of Viewing Copies Supplement (1974)*; *Viewing Catalogue of Fiction Films*—revised every other year (1983 edition in preparation); *Catalogue. Volume 1. Non Fiction Films (1980)*; *Catalogue of Stills, Posters and Designs (1982)*—lists 40,000 titles for which stills, posters and set designs are held in the Stills Collection.

The computerisation of the Archive's film records began in August 1979 employing a system developed by Bemrose Information Services of Derby. The first stage of the programme required that the records of 10,000 non-fiction films be stored on computer tape, making it possible to produce photo-typeset pages of text, arranged by country and date, and a complete title index and subject index automatically.

The 1980 volume of over 800 pages plus illustrations is available from the National Film Archive at £50 (plus post and packaging).

access

1. *Cataloguing Section*: All catalogues can be consulted (preferably by prior appointment) on the Archive's premises at 81 Dean Street, London W1, or alternatively the Section will answer written and telephone enquiries.

2. *Viewing Service*: The Viewing Service caters for private viewings by *bona fide* researchers and students viewing course-related material on the Archive's premises (for which a small handling fee is charged). The Archive's viewing print collection is by no means complete, but a continuous, systematic copying programme ensures that most actual and potential demands are met. The Viewings Supervisor, who arranges access to the Archive's film and television collections, is available for consultation at 81 Dean Street, London W1, Monday to Friday, between 10.30 and 17.30.

3. *Production Library*: This service has been developed to supply extracts of Archive films to film-makers, TV producers and the like for use in compilations and other projects *where no other source exists*. Enquiries should be made to the Production Librarian at 81 Dean Street, who will arrange catalogue consultation, viewing, marking up and processing and provide a full scale of charges on request. Copyright clearance has to be obtained in writing before material can be supplied.

4. *Stills, Posters and Designs*: The Stills Collection, for which the Archive has curatorial responsibility, is one of the largest and most comprehensive in the world, a unique research tool consisting of over 2,000,000 black and white stills representing more than 40,000 film titles and 9,500 individual actors and actresses. These are housed in seven modern electronic storage and retrieval systems which permit rapid search and access. The collection also contains 200,000 colour transparencies, 8,000 posters and 800 original set designs. For reasons of quality and economy, and the need to set up a programme to preserve the entire collection by copying it on to master negatives, the Archive has established its own photographic studio based at Ernest Lindgren House, Berkhamsted. One of the functions of the studio is to supply copy stills for use in research, publishing, etc.

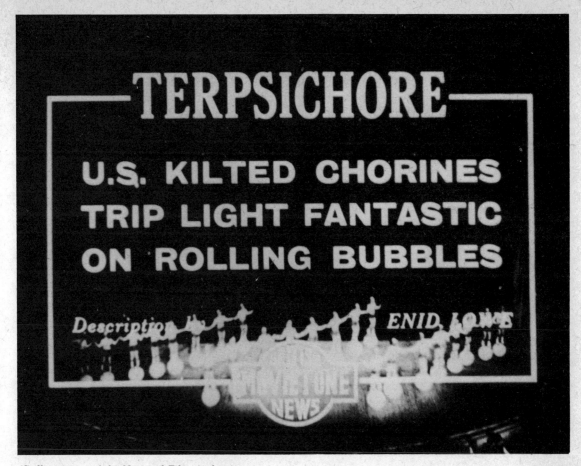

(Still courtesy of the National Film Archive)

These can be ordered by personal visit (by prior appointment) or by post from the Stills, Posters and Designs Collection, 81 Dean Street, London W1, where details of prices can also be obtained.

THORN-EMI PATHÉ LIBRARY

addresses	Thorn-EMI Elstree Studios Limited, Shenley Road, Borehamwood WD6 1JG, Herts.
	Tel: 01-953 1600
	and
	20 St Anne's Court, London W1
	Tel: 01-437 0444
contact	Mr G. Marshall, Head of Library Services (Elstree)
history	*Pathé's Animated Gazette*—started regular bi-weekly publication in London in February 1910. The length of the newsreel at the time was about 300 feet and by 1914 ninety copies were being printed. In 1914 up to the start of World War 1 a daily edition was issued. In the years after, the length and number of copies increased gradually and for several years two newsreels were published weekly, a long one of 600–700 feet and a short one of 300 feet.

Pathé Super Sound Gazette: Pathé Super Gazette: & Pathé Gazette—with the advent of sound in 1930 Pathé had to publish the above three newsreels to cover the period when cinemas were changing from silent to sound projectors. After some years, the first two were discontinued. *Pathé Gazette* continued until the end of 1945.

Pathé News—this was the new title given to the Pathé newsreel from newsreel number 1, 1946. In 1960 *Pathé News* produced its first reels in colour. The last release of the newsreel was no. 70–71, 26 February 1970.

Pathé Pictorial—first released in March 1918 this cinemagazine continued in production until 27 March 1969.

Eve's Film Review—this newsmagazine for women began in 1921 and continued until 1933.

Pathétone Weekly—this international production was first released weekly in 1930 with a view to incorporating all the semi-news events which passed into the Pathé organisation and its news exchanges around the world. It ceased production in 1941.

Astra Gazette—a digest of mainly *Pathé Pictorial* material that was compiled for the RAF. Twelve gazettes were issued.

Thames Television 'out-takes'—the Library acquired these by arrangement with Thames from 1973 to 1981. (Some 25% of total footage received has been kept.)

Total estimated footage is 50 million feet. Thorn-EMI is co-operating with the Imperial War Museum and the National Film Archive on a huge preservation programme. The IWM will start with films of the World War 1 period and the NFA in 1919. The nitrate originals will be cleaned, copied and re-catalogued. The programme, which will continue for many years, will be an important contribution to newsfilm records of the twentieth century.

components Can be original negatives, dupe negatives, fine grain or lavender masters—whatever format the film originally arrived on. All pre-World War 1 material has been transferred to safety stock.

storage All the film in the collection is stored in temperature-controlled vaults at the Thorn-EMI Elstree Studios, Borehamwood, Hertfordshire.

cataloguing *The Card Catalogue*—this main catalogue is divided into two separate sections, 1) Pre-War (but including the World War 2 period) and 2) Post-War. In-house subject headings are used for the subject section of the catalogue and there is also a personality file. No footage is included on the catalogue cards—Pathé regrets this now but a decision was never taken to include this piece of information (for issued material it is recorded on the issue sheets).

Pathé Colour Pictorial Card Index—this is filed in fireproof metal cabinets with the main card catalogue. The cataloguing of this material is on a shot for shot basis rather than a story basis from 1960.

There is a microfiche at Elstree Studios of all the Index Cards so reference work can be done at both sites. Microform copies are available for purchase in either fiche or film.

documentation Issue sheets for *Pathé Super Sound Gazette, Pathé Super Gazette, Pathé Gazette, Pathé News, Pathé Pictorial, Eve's Film Review, Pathétone Weekly* and *Astra Gazette*. Pathé 'Old Neg' folder—this Twinlock folder lists some 2,500 unissued stories from the World War 1 period which are not recorded in the main card catalogue. *Cameraman's dope sheets*—these are stored in various metal cabinets with, in many cases, relevant newspaper clippings, music cue sheets, programmes, handout literature, etc. Cameraman's dope sheets and associated literature for newsreel material have only been kept since the mid 1950s. Dope sheets for *Pathé Pictorial* have been kept since 1950. *Shot lists*—these have been retained from 1940 onwards. *'Unused' file*—this documentation, recording details of unissued films, is stored in various metal cabinets. *Commentary sheets*—there are, of course, no commentary sheets for the silent period. At least half of those from the 1930s have been kept. *Shooting scripts*—these were acquired from Thames Television under the arrangement that this company had with EMI-Pathé for the latter to take Thames' 'out-takes'. Only some scripts were received, more often the material was just accompanied by a brief note. *Television shot lists*—these are shot lists of television programmes such as 'Time to Remember', 'The Peaceful Years', etc. in which Pathé material has been used.

access   There is no charge for consulting the catalogues and issue sheets. Charges are levied for viewing and copying. There is an initial charge for viewing five items after which there is a fee for every item subsequently viewed. Viewing time is charged by the hour. For copying there is a 20ft minimum charge. However, there are special rates for different types of user. Commercial firms pay the highest fee followed by television companies. Educational and government bodies pay the cheapest rate.

The Hindenburg airship disaster 1937 (still courtesy of Thorn-EMI Pathé)

VISNEWS FILM LIBRARY

Visnews Ltd., Cumberland Avenue, London NW10 7EH

Tel: 01-965 7733

contact   Pam Turner, Library Manager

history   Visnews, the international television news agency, provides a daily syndicated news service to 275 broadcasters in 88 countries. The agency is jointly owned by the British Broadcasting Corporation, Reuters, the Australian Broadcasting Commission, the Canadian Broadcasting Corporation and the Broadcasting Corporation of New Zealand.

A network of cameramen, staff and stringers, numbering approximately 400, works for Visnews throughout the world. In addition, Visnews has access to all news material shot by its owner-organisations and also by the National Broadcasting Company of America, with which Visnews has a close working agreement. Special arrangements also exist for acquiring news material from television organisations in Africa, Eastern and Western Europe, South America, China, Japan and elsewhere. All this material, together with that from other sources, ultimately finds its way into the Visnews Film Library.

In addition to its own archives, the Library owns the following newsreel libraries: *Gaumont Graphic* 1910–1933; *Empire News Bulletin* 1926–1930; *Gaumont-British News* 1929–1959; *Universal News* 1930–1949; *British Paramount News* 1931–1957. All newsreel material is on 35mm safety stock (but see below under storage facilities) other material on 16mm film or videotape.

holdings   The total footage, dating back to 1896, is some 40 million feet, growing at a rate of something like 500,000 feet of 16mm colour film or videotape a year.

components   16mm film—b/w or colour, 35mm safety b/w neg. and pos., 2″ b/w video tape, 1″ colour video tape.

storage   Most of the Visnews collection is stored in the Library. An exception is the nitrate material in the early newsreel libraries. Much of this film was transferred onto 2″ videotape with $^1/_2$″ copies being made available for viewing purposes at the Library. All the nitrate material was then deposited at the National Film Archive and the Imperial War Museum—the latter received mainly the material covering the periods 1914–1918 and 1939–1945. All the newsreel acetate film has been kept at the Visnews Library. Stock is kept in the Library on roller shelving in an open plan area.

cataloguing   **Visnews** *The card catalogue*—this is arranged under counttry and date, location, personality and subject. The country and date section is the master file: films are listed by country and then by production number order, which is a quick date guide as the higher the number the more recent the accession in a given year. The subject headings used are based in part on 'Sears List of Subject Headings' and on the Universal Decimal Classification.

Newsreel libraries: *Gaumont British dictionary catalogue*— a card catalogue. *Gaumont Graphic card catalogue. British Paramount News card index*—this is in three sections—location, personality and subject. Cards contain shot lists also. *Universal News dictionary catalogue*—a card catalogue.

documentation **Visnews:** Production sheet—this is a permanent record of the provenance of the material, the used title, the film stock, whom serviced, how many prints made, etc. The last three years' sheets are kept in the Library for quick reference, the earliest years are filed in a storeroom. Editor's dope sheet/shot list—also contains transcript of commentary. The permanent record is on microfilm. The sheets are destroyed once they have been microfilmed, which is normally after a period of one year.

Weekly summary of material available for daily shipment—this summary is sent out to subscribers. Subject headings authority file. Junking records in the form of inter-office memos.

Newsreel libraries: Issue sheets for *Gaumont Graphic* (1913–1925), *Gaumont-British News* (1934–1959). *Empire News Bulletin* (1926–1932), *Universal News* (1930–1956) and *British Paramount News* (1931–1957).

Gaumont-British News ledgers (1930–1949).

Gaumont Graphic accession books—a handwritten record. (The *Gaumont Graphic* dope sheets appear to be lost).

Empire News Bulletin notebook of accessions—a small thick handwritten record.

British Paramount News accession books. An original handwritten record in three hardback notebooks. Also contains details of unusued material. *British Paramount News* dope sheets.

Universal News accession books.

Video selected list. This lists in notebook form the newsreel nitrate material that has been transferred to video.

Video roll file—this is a record in typed form of the newsreel stories that each video roll contains.

junking   Items serviced to subscribers are never junked. Other non-serviced items are selected for retention. Records of junked material are kept. The Film Librarian regularly notifies by memo the relevant section of Visnews as to what material has been accepted by the Library and what has been rejected. Material may be rejected because of poor physical quality or because the Library already holds the same story from another source.

access   There is no charge for consulting the catalogues, the only restriction being the number of people that can work on the catalogues at any one time. As soon as the researcher views material normal service charges apply. There is no discount for educational bodies. (The Library has no viewing prints and is, consequently, always screening master material). A list of charges is available from the Library.

Documentation Centres

BBC WRITTEN ARCHIVES CENTRE

Caversham Park, Reading, Berks. RG4 8TZ

Tel: 0734 472742. Exts. 280/281/282

contact	Written Archives Officer: Mrs. J. M. Kavanagh
function	The purpose of the Centre is to make information available from its holdings both to BBC staff and to non-BBC researchers.
holdings	200,000 files covering every aspect of the BBC's work from 1922 to 1962. Areas covered include television from its earliest period, news, wartime broadcasting, music, variety, drama, education and religious broadcasting. Files relating to news cover policy for both radio and television with specific files (1935–1956) on the *Television Newsreel* (see below). There is an extensive collection of press cuttings.
access	Papers are available for research, with certain limitations, up to 1962. Researchers intending to visit the Centre are asked to write well in advance giving details of the subject of their research. Charges are made for certain services.
special note	THE BBC TELEVISION NEWSREEL

It was clear by June 1946 when the Television Service re-opened after the War, that the Newsreel Association of Great Britain were determined not to make the cinema newsreels available to Television as they had done pre-war. It was decided, accordingly, to put a BBC Television Newsreel into production as soon as a unit could be recruited and trained, the necessary equipment purchased and arrangements concluded with American Television and foreign commercial film-makers for the shooting of overseas coverage.

An Exchange Agreement was made with N.B.C., individual firms and free-lance cameramen throughout the world were signed up and the first edition of a bi-weekly fifteen minute BBC Television Newsreel was televised on 5 January, 1948, 'dubbing' being carried out for the first few editions at the Warner Brothers' Studios at Teddington and, later, in the R. C. A. Recording Theatre in Hammersmith.

With the commissioning of the BBC's Dubbing Theatre at Alexandra Palace in August, 1949, it was possible to record in the early afternoon of the day of issue instead of in the morning, and with the equipping of that Theatre and of the Telecine equipment with magnetic-film recording and reproducing facilities in August, 1951, dubbing could be further deferred until two hours before transmission thus making it practicable to bring the sound-track of a given edition right up to date even though the picture had been shot hours if not days beforehand.

Television Newsreel was increased to three editions a week in December 1950 and to five editions a week in June 1952. It was at this stage that the existence of Television Newsreel started really seriously to worry the Film Industry.

During the course of its 1,078 editions spread over six and a half years, Television Newsreel carried some 6,500 stories of which nearly half were shot by staff cameramen, several of whom were despatched as far afield as Korea, Malaya and Kenya. Exceptionally, short-term agreements were concluded with the Newsreel Association of Great Britain whereby the BBC had access to their coverage of, for example, a Royal Tour.

The original agreement with N.B.C. proved, unhappily, to mean virtually one-way traffic from London to New York, so this was abandoned in 1953 so that the BBC could be free to buy from (and to sell to) the Columbia Broadcasting System and Telenews—this resulting in a much faster service from the BBC's angle.

It is difficult to give 'typical' samples of the more outstanding stories covered by Newsreel, but they have included the Silver Wedding of King George VI and later his death and his funeral; the births of Prince Charles and Princess Anne; the accession and Coronation of Elizabeth II; two General Elections; two American Presidential elections; the Korea War from beginning to end, and fighting in Greece, Palestine, Malaya, Indo-China and Kenya; the Berlin Airlift; the Atlantic Pact; the Flying Enterprise; the Affray; and the floods of Lynmouth and the East Coast; sport ranging through the 1948 and the 1952 Olympic Games. The first sensational 'scoop' was the Helicopter relief of Wolf Rock lighthouse in early 1948—one of the last was the Bannister Four Minute Mile from start to finish.

The last edition of Television Newsreel was televised on 2 July last [1954] and the following are extracts from the commentary of the last story in this edition.

'Six and a half years ago, on January the 4th, 1948, the barque 'Pamir' sailed across the television screens of the country . . . these pictures of her arrival were the first item in the first edition of Television Newsreel . . . Today the Pamir is brought back to Television screens, today . . . 1,077 editions after her first appearance—the Pamir forms the last item in the last edition of Television Newsreel in its present form . . . Young sailors of the future will come to regard her as a monument to an illustrious past and an example to those who follow'.

[Special note reproduced by kind permission of the BBC].

BRITISH FILM INSTITUTE LIBRARY SERVICES

127 Charing Cross Road, London WC2H 0EA

Tel: 01-437 4355

contact	Librarian: Sandra Archer Information Officer: Peter Seward
function	The cinema collection is international in scope but there is a special emphasis on British cinema. The television service is largely concerned with British broadcast television.
holdings	**Books**—32,000 (one third in duplicate) on all aspects of film and television. Catalogues by author, title and classified by subject (own system, based on UDC).
	Periodicals—450 titles currently received. Indexed by title, personality and general subjects. Many journals available on roll microfilm.
	Scripts—6,000 film scripts, 600 television scripts.
	Newspaper clippings—collection from late thirties to date, mainly from the British daily and weekly press. Classified by title, personality and general subjects. Title and personality material available in microjackets.
	Programmes and press books—an extensive collection of press books, campaign books and handouts mainly relating to the British and American industries from the silent period to the present. Cataloguing in progress.
	Sound recordings—a small collection of tapes, mainly interviews with film-makers. A few film soundtracks. Interim catalogue available.
	Festivals—an extensive collection of film festival programmes, leaflets and clippings covering all major film festivals from 1934 to the present.

Special collections—mainly documentation relating to the work of individuals, including scrapbooks, diaries and memorabilia, but also including the *British Board of Film Censors Collection.*

There are three special collections of **newsreel documentation:**

Stanley J. 'Percy' Mumford Collection—this collection of material from the newsreel cameraman includes, for example, a 45-page foolscap typescript, *Forty years behind a movie camera: interesting highlights of my experiences in the industry*, written in 1949; newspaper clippings; 2 tape recordings; *Universal News* identity card; British War Correspondent's Licence Number card, etc. (Library reference: Bay 1. Special Collections Room)

Patrick Wyand Collection—This collection of material from the *British Movietone News* cameraman includes, for example, a typescript listing all of Wyand's assignments from 1934–1974; Regulations for War Correspondents 1944; British War Correspondent's Licence Number card, etc. (Library reference: Bay 3. Special Collections Room).

Two handbills for the Pathé Mobile News Cinema aboard L.N.E.R. trains, 1936 and 1937. (Library reference: Single documents, no. 46. Special Collections Room.)

A detailed schedule of all items in the individual collections may be consulted at the Library Reading Room.

Television—broadly the aim is to provide a service on British broadcast television parallel to and integrated with that already available on cinema. Books, scripts and other related material are being collected and catalogued. Programme journals and other publications are being indexed by programme title, personality and general subject. Eventually it is hoped that the Department may become the initial national reference centre for information on TV while promoting ease of access to collections held by broadcasting organisations and other institutions.

access   All services are accessible to the public by letter, telephone or personal visit but regular users are expected to take out membership of the BFI.

SLADE FILM HISTORY REGISTER

c/o British Universities Film & Video Council, 55 Greek Street, London W1V 5LR

Tel: 01-734 3687/8

contact   James Ballantyne

history   The Slade Film History Register was established in 1969 at the instigation of Thorold Dickinson, then Professor of Film at the Slade School of Fine Art, University College London, with the aid of a grant from the Social Science Research Council. In exploring the organisation and use of film and other audio-visual material for historical studies, the object was to create a central register of film material likely to be of interest to historians in much the same way as the National Register of Archives had done for the country's primary written documents. The Register was to concentrate on film material and only incidentally to include still photographs and sound recordings for the period 1895 to 1962, ending at the point at which the British National Film Catalogue began in 1963.

The Social Science Research Council's grant came to an end in 1973 but University College continued to support the Register until May 1975, the last eight months in conjunction with the British Universities Film Council. By June 1975, it had become clear that University College's financial position would not permit the Register's work to continue and its staff had to disperse. Since the Council's work had close affinity with that of the Register, University College agreed to transfer all the Register's assets to the British Universities Film Council with the approval of the Social Science Research Council. All cataloguing and indexing activities ceased at this stage owing to a lack of funds and subsequently the Council has only been able to maintain an enquiry service and to add some further documentation and literature to the Register's reference library.

At the beginning of 1976 a Working Party was established to review the Register's functions and advise on its future development. The Working Party reported in October 1977 and among its recommendations were the following: the original aim of the Register 'to provide a central register of film material in much the same way as the National Register of Archives has done for written documents' should be upheld, with the addition that television materials should also be included; the Register should record the scope and major strengths of all film and television collections in Great Britain, including those in private hands; the Register should aim to produce a directory of film and television collections in the United Kingdom as soon as a sufficient body of relevant information had been accumulated (see *Researcher's Guide to British Film & Television Collections*).

holdings

Book Stock—280 volumes

Periodicals—3 are currently taken including *Television News Index and Abstracts* (Vanderbilt Television News Archive)

Newsreel documentation—the following items have been copied:

British Movietone News issue sheets	1929–1979
British Paramount News issue sheets	1931–1957
Empire News Bulletin issue sheets	1926–1932
Gaumont-British News issue sheets	1934–1959
Gaumont-British News ledgers	1930–1949
Gaumont Graphic issue sheets	1913–1925
Pathé Gazette issue sheets	1919–1947
Pathé News issue sheets	1948–1970
Universal Talking News issue sheets	1930–1956

Cinemagazine documentation—the following items have been copied:

British Movietone's 'Look at Life' series title index	
Eve's Film Review issue sheets	1921–1933
Pathé Pictorial issue sheets	1918–1969
Pathétone Weekly issue sheets	1930–1941
Warwork News issue sheets	1942–1945

In addition, there are copies of such items as the Pathé list of early newsreel material covering the years 1895–1917, the lists of French and Soviet World War 2 newsreels held in the Imperial War Museum, a list of the German feature films produced between 1933 and 1945, a list of Library of Congress World War 2 German material; Visnews weekly summaries of colour film available for daily shipment, from November 1977, and so on. Numerous published film catalogues and pamphlets and articles relating to film and history have also been accumulated.

The card catalogue of British newsreel film—this lists some 30,000 selected newsreel stories, one-third of which have been classified by the Universal Decimal Classification scheme; the other two-thirds still awaiting classification are arranged chronologically under newsreel company.

The card catalogue of documentary and non-fiction film—this lists in alphabetical order by title, some 6,000 selected items produced between the years 1914 and 1960.

Appendix 1

a) A typical newsreel issue sheet

```
BRITISH MOVIETONE NEWS.  VOL. 20.  NO. 1035.

              Released:- 4. 4. 49.
              -----------------


MOVIETONE'S NEWS - reported by LESLIE MITCHELL.

              TITLES.                                    30.

PRINCESSES' ENGAGEMENTS.

PRINCESS MARGARET visits a Nurses Training School
in Bristol.                                             40.
PRINCESS ELIZABETH and the DUKE OF EDINBURGH
open a new lock on the Mersey and later make
a tour of Liverpool Cathedral.                         136.

JUNGLE IS BARRIER ON REBEL ROUND-UP.

British troops and planes of the R.A.F. attack
a bandit hide-out in Malaya, killing and wounding
some, taking one prisoner.                             110.

POLITICIANS ABROAD.

Mr. Eden arrives home after his tour of the
empire which included India, Australia and
New Zealand finally returning to Heathrow.              94.

Mr Churchill is welcomed in Washington by
President Truman.                                       40.

Mr. Bevin, with other Foriegn Ministers, is
greeted on arrival at New York to sign the
Atlantic Pact.                                          50.

A PEACE CONFERENCE IN NEW YORK.

In New York, Americans picket the Waldorf
while inside Soviet propagandists attend
a "Peace" Conference. At the Madison Square
Garden, Americans donate dollars to the
Communist cause amid much activity.                    82.

GERDAN K.O'S. TURPIN.

At the Empress Hall, London, Marcel Cerdan,
World Middleweight champion, knocks out, in the
seventh round, Dick Turpin, the British and
Empire Middleweight Champion.                          154.

                                                       736.
```

(Reproduced by kind permission of British Movietonews)

b) A typical cinemagazine issue sheet

PATHE SOUND PICTORIAL NO. 731   RELEASED 7. 4. 32.

COACHING UP TO DATE
The rowing season is on, and here's
the novel way they train the college
crews on the Schuylkill River.   130 feet

ALONG AUSTRALIA'S BARRIER REEF
This most famous of coral reefs, skirts
the north-eastern coast of the great
island Continent for 1,000 miles. Built
by tiny marine organisms, its origin
remains shrouded in mystery.   280 feet

THE WEAKER SEX
Meet Sansonia, the world's strongest
woman. Sansonia is just as strong
indoors as outdoors, and this multiple
expander is just a pastime to her.   200 feet

A WONDERFUL BIRD IS THE PELICAN
Lots of us have heard the verse about
the Pelican - but if you don't believe
all about its bill, here's a picture
to convince you.   150 feet

GERALDO
Introducing this famous conductor, and
his Gauchos Tango Orchestra from the
Savoy Hotel, in "Carmelita".   320 feet

(Reproduced by kind permission of Thorn-EMI Pathé)

Appendix 2

Some early catalogues of topical films held by the National Film Archive Cataloguing Department

[Hepworth] *Hepwix films for the cinematograph.* London: Hepworth Manufacturing Company, 1903. 64p.

Lists some topical material including the funeral of Queen Victoria.

[Hepworth] *Hepwix films for the cinematograph.* London: Hepworth Manufacturing Company, 1906. 141p.

Lists some topical material.

Kineto Film List 1912. London: Kineto Ltd., 1912. 91p.

Lists topical, travel, educational films, etc.

[Paul] *Illustrated catalogue of a new & original series of standard-sized animated photograph films: list no. 15, August 1898.* London: Robert W. Paul, 1898. 32p.

Lists some topical material.

[Paul] *Catalogue of Paul's animatographs & films.* London: Robert W. Paul, 1901. (102)p.

Lists some topical material, e.g. Derby, Boat Race, Cowes.

[Paul] *Catalogue of Paul's animatographs & films.* London: Robert W. Paul, 1902. (104)p.

Lists topical material.

[Paul] *Catalogue of selected animated photograph films. Section B: 1906-7.* London: Robert W. Paul, 1906. 88p.

Lists topical material.

[*Urban Films Catalogue Supplements 1902-8*] London: Charles Urban Trading Co., 1902-8. Various pagination.

Lists topical material.

[*Urban Films Catalogue Supplements 1904*]. London: Charles Urban Trading Co., 1904. (Supplement no. 1, January, 52p. Supplement no. 2, March, 8p.)

Lists topical material.

[Urban Films] *Revised list of high-class original copyrighted Bioscope Films.* London: Charles Urban Trading Co., February 1905. 337p.

Early topical material '. . . depicting scenes from all countries'.

[Urban Films] *Catalogue of exclusively educational and scientific subjects.* London: Charles Urban Trading Co., 1908. 252p.

As title including topical material.

[Urban Films] *General catalogue of classified subjects.* London: Charles Urban Trading Co., 1909. 432p.

Lists 'Urban', 'Eclipse', 'Radios' film subjects and 'Urbanora' educational series. Topical material.

Walturdaw catalogues 1904-1911 (including the 'Walturdaw' Lending Library of Bioscope Pictures, List no. 14, 1904 and The 'Walturdaw' Animated Pictures catalogue, 1907). London: The 'Walturdaw' Co. 133p.

Lists some topical items.

Warwick Trading Company Catalogue 1901. London: Warwick Trading Company. 224p.

Lists topical material.

Warwick Trading Company Catalogue Supplement no. 1. London: Warwick Trading Company, August 1901. p.223-86.

Lists topical material.

[Warwick] *Blue book of 'Warwick' and 'Star' selected film subjects.* London: Warwick Trading Company, 1902. 143p.

Lists topical material.

[Warwick] *Film blue book supplements nos. 1-3, 1902.* London: Warwick Trading Company, 1902. Various pagination.

Supplement no. 1 deals with the Coronation of King Edward VII.

Appendix 3

Films and Videos about the British newsreels

ARCHIVE SERIES. NO. 1: NEVILLE CHAMBERLAIN
dist.: Higher Education Film & Video Library, Hire or Sale;
1975: p.i.: University of Leeds Television Service and
University of Leeds, School of History: auth. Prof. D. Dilks,
A. Beattie, N. Pronay.
Film. 16mm. sd. b&w. 27min.
Eight newsreel stories featuring Neville Chamberlain, from the 1930s,
with identifying titles. Chamberlain comments on the Labour Budget,
1931; explains Tariff Bill, 1932; expounds 1936 budget; on national
health and the aspirations of the people; special newsreel issue after
Munich, 1938; on appeasement, 1938; on dangers of war, June 1939;
as war leader, Mansion House speech, Jan. 1940. Notes: Copies of
supplementary 22-page booklet are supplied with each film; in this the
authors discuss the significance of each particular newsreel.
Restrictions on use: Only for use within the purchasing educational
institution. Other versions available; Video cassette (Sale only).
Standard formats. Item number: 3HE 426.—Intended audience:
Undergraduates.

ARCHIVE SERIES. NO. 2: THE ORIGINS OF THE
COLD WAR
dist.: Higher Education Film & Video Library, Hire or Sale;
1976: p.i.: InterUniversity History Film Consortium and
University of Nottingham, Department of American Studies:
comp., auth. Peter G. Boyle.
Film. 16mm. sd. b&w. 28min.
A selection of unedited British newsreel stories relating to the theme of
the Cold War. Each item is identified by title, source and date:
Churchill's Iron Curtain speech: Truman's Doctrine speech; Marshall
Plan; Eastern Europe survey 1945–8; Formation of NATO; Berlin
Blockade; Acheson on atomic weapons; Korean War. Archival
material from Visnews. 16-page booklet supplied with each copy of
the film. Other versions available: Video cassette (Sale only). Item
number: 2HE 247—Intended audience: Undergraduates in history.
Restrictions on use: only for use in purchasing educational institution.

ARCHIVE SERIES. NO. 3: STANLEY BALDWIN
dist.: Higher Education Film & Video Library, Hire or Sale;
1979: p.i.: InterUniversity History Film Consortium and
University of London Audio-Visual Centre for University of
London, Queen Mary College: auth. Dr John Ramsden.
Film. 16mm. sd. b&w. 45min.
A selection of the major newsreel and Conservative Party Film Unit
productions in which Stanley Baldwin appeared between 1925 and
1935. Notes: Copies of a 21-page booklet by Dr Ramsden are supplied
with each film. Also available on video cassette (Sale only). Item
number: HE 428.—Restrictions on use: Only for viewing within the
purchasing educational institution

BEFORE HINDSIGHT
dist.: British Film Institute Film & Video Library, Hire; 1977:
p.c.: Metropolis Pictures with British Film Institute Production Board. exec.p. Elizabeth Taylor-Mead. d. Jonathan
Lewis. sc. Jonathan Lewis, Elizabeth Taylor-Mead. ph.
Roger Deakins, ed. Jonathan Lewis. res. Elizabeth Taylor-
Mead. nar. James Cameron. collaborators: Hugh Cuth-
bertson, Stanley Forman, Bert Hogenkamp, Victoria Wegg-
Prosser, Herbert Maiden.
Film. 16mm. sd. b&w/col. 78min.
Uses newsreels from British Movietone, Gaumont-British, Paramount
and Universal as well as material from the *March of Time* and the Film
and Photo League to illustrate its thesis that the British reels were
regarded in the thirties primarily as uncontroversial programme-
fillers. Among those interviewed as Gerald Sanger, Leslie Mitchell,
George Elvin, Edgar Anstey, and Ivor Montague.

FILM AS EVIDENCE. PART 1: BEFORE YOUR VERY
EYES
dist.: BBC Television Enterprises Film Sales, Sale; 1976: p.c.:
BBC Continuing Education Television. p. Howard Smith. sc.
Nicholas Pronay.
Film. 16mm. sd. b&w. 25min.
For nearly 25 years the twice weekly cinema newsreel was regularly
seen by more than 20 million people, and for the vast majority it was
their first look at the world outside their own restricted horizons. The
newsreels were therefore one—some would say the most—important
influence shaping public opinion about the outside world. The cinema
also provided thousands of screens on which politicians could appeal
directly to millions of ordinary people—it was, in fact, the beginning
of a new age of political mass communications. The main purpose of
the series (which consists largely of extracts from the newsreels) is to
examine the reels in this light—to investigate what information is
provided or not provided and in which form—to see what is being said
and why. Part 1 looks first at the cinema newsreels in general and then
concentrates on the ways in which, in the later thirties, they dealt with
the important, controversial and very unpopular issue of rearmament.
Intended audience: general without previous knowledge of the
subject, though with some interest in understanding the background
to current affairs.

FILM AS EVIDENCE. PART 2: TOMORROW THE
WORLD
dist.: BBC Television Enterprises Film Sales, Sale; 1976: p.c.:
BBC Continuing Education Television. p. Howard Smith. sc.
Nicholas Pronay, Prof. John Grenville.
Film. 16mm. sd. b&w. 25min.
Examines the way in which the newsreel's view of Hitler's Germany
changed. It begins with the images of Germany presented in the silent
newsreel, continues with the uncertainties following Hitler's rise to
power in 1933 and the growing hostility of the later thirties and ends
with the uncompromising propagandist view of 1940 and after.

FILM AS EVIDENCE. PART 3: SOMETHING HAS TO
BE DONE
dist.: BBC Television Enterprises Film Sales, Sale; 1976: p.c.:
BBC Continuing Education Television. p. Howard Smith. sc.
Nicholas Pronay.
Film. 16mm. sd. b&w. 25min.
Continues the story begun in the previous film. It investigates the way
in which the attitude of grim satisfaction at Germany's total defeat,
and at the just consequences of that defeat for the German people,
which prevailed in 1945, was quickly transformed into the conviction
that the Germans must be allowed to win their way back to
membership of the civilised world.

FILM AS EVIDENCE. Part 4: WE WERE RIGHT
dist.: BBC Television Enterprises Film Sales, Sale; 1976: p.c.:
BBC Continuing Education Television. p. Howard Smith, sc.
Nicholas Pronay.
Film. 16mm. sd. b&w. 25min.
The nationalisation of the Suez Canal in July 1956 and the subsequent
invasion of Egypt by British and French forces in November 1956 was
the last great international crisis before television replaced the cinema
newsreel as the public's main source of information about the outside
world. This film questions how effectively the newsreels were able to
reflect the fierce passions which the crisis aroused.

FILM AS EVIDENCE. PART 5: MEN OF THE HOUR
dist.: BBC Television Enterprises Film Sales, Sale; 1976; p.c.: BBC Continuing Education Television. p. Howard Smith. sc. Nicholas Pronay.
Film. 16mm. sd. b&w. 25 min.
Looks first at the way in which the newsreels reported the 1935 election campaign, and then concentrates on the way in which Neville Chamberlain first mastered the techniques of this new medium of mass communication, and then reaped his reward in the way newsreels covered the Munich crisis of 1938.

GUERNICA—THE MAKING OF A MYTH
dist.: Open University Educational Enterprises, Off-air recording licence or Sale; 1982: p.c.: British Broadcasting Corporation, Open University Productions: auth., pres. Dr Anthony Aldgate. (Inquiry course)
Film. 16mm. sd. b&w/col. 25 min.
Contrasts the newsreel coverage of the bombing of Guernica from both a German and British point of view. Dr Aldgate of the Open University analyses their use of sound and picture in the context of their contemporary presentation. He discusses with a German television producer the extent to which the newsreel film accurately reflects contemporary attitudes, and the extent to which it might change current opinions.

HISTORY THROUGH THE NEWSREEL—THE 1930s. PART 1: THE NEWS AND THE NEWSREEL
dist.: Macmillan Education Hirings, Hire or Sale; 1976: p.c.: Macmillan Education for Historical Association.
Film. 16mm. sd. b&w. 15 min.
Credits: lect. Nicholas Pronay, Peter Wenham. series ed. Nicholas Pronay. Advisory Board: Prof. J. A. S. Grenville, Prof. H. Hearder, Brian Haworth, Prof. A. Marwick, John Standen, Peter Wenham.
An introduction to the 4-part series with a short summary of the social context of the British newsreels, including photographs of contemporary cinemas and figures for cinema attendances, followed by a complete newsreel—Gaumont-British, March 30, 1939. Note: Accompanied by a 32-page booklet, 'Notes for Teachers', which contains an introductory essay, detailed comments on the newsreel material, a transcript of the soundtrack and a bibliography.

HISTORY THROUGH THE NEWSREEL—THE 1930s. PART 2: THE UNEMPLOYED
dist.: Macmillan Education Hirings, Hire or Sale; 1976: p.c.: Macmillan Education for Historical Association.
Film. 16mm. sd. b&w. 15 min.
Credits: lect. Prof. Arthur Marwick. series ed. Nicholas Pronay. Advisory Board: Prof. J. A. S. Grenville, Prof. H. Hearder, Brian Haworth, Prof. A. Marwick, John Standen, Peter Wenham.
Brings together various newsreel stories about the marches of the unemployed in the 1930s and the official responses to the crisis. Note: Accompanied by a 32.page booklet, 'Notes for Teachers', which contains an introductory essay, detailed comments on the newsreel material, a transcript of the soundtrack and a bibliography.

HISTORY THROUGH THE NEWSREEL—THE 1930s. PART 3: NAZI GERMANY
dist.: Macmillan Education Hirings, Hire or Sale; 1976: p.c.: Macmillan Education for Historical Association.
Film. 16mm. sd. b&w. 15 min.
Credits: lect. Prof. J. A. S. Grenville. series ed. Nicholas Pronay. Advisory Board: Prof. J. A. S. Grenville, Prof. H. Hearder, Brian Haworth, Prof. A. Marwick, John Standen, Peter Wenham.
How the British newsreels' treatment of Nazi Germany altered during the 1930s, from stressing Hitler's legitimacy and the Christianity of the Nazis to the bitter response noted in the final stories. Note: Accompanied by a 32-page booklet, 'Notes for Teachers', which contains an introductory essay, detailed comments on the newsreel material, a transcript of the soundtrack and a bibliography.

HISTORY THROUGH THE NEWSREEL—THE 1930s. PART 4: IF WAR SHOULD COME
dist.: Macmillan Education Hirings, Hire or Sale; 1976: p.c.: Macmillan Education for Historical Association.
Film. 16mm. sd. b&w. 15 min.
Credits: lect. Dr R. A. C. Parker. series ed. Nicholas Pronay. Advisory Board: Prof. J. A. S. Grenville, Prof. H. Hearder, Brian Haworth, Prof. A. Marwick, John Standen, Peter Wenham.
The British newsreels' coverage of war preparations—interspersed with government propaganda—at the end of the 1930s. Note: Accompanied by a 32-page booklet, 'Notes for Teachers', which contains an introductory essay, detailed comments on the newsreel material, a transcript of the soundtrack and a bibliography.

ILLUSIONS OF REALITY. PART 1: WINDOW ON THE WORLD
dist.: BBC Television Enterprises Film Sales, Sale; 1979: p.c.: BBC Continuing Education Television. p. Howard Smith. sc. Nicholas Pronay.
Film. 16mm. sd. b&w. 25 min.
This series examines the value as historical evidence of cinema newsreels, documentaries and television news from the thirties to the present day. The main purpose of the series (which consists largely of extracts from newsreels and documentaries) is to examine the reels in this light—to investigate what information is provided or not provided and in which form—to see what is being said and why. Part 1 looks at the cinema newsreels in general. What kind of outside world did the British public see, on film, for the first time? Intended audience: general, and for use in the support of media studies.

ILLUSIONS OF REALITY. PART 2: MEN OF THE HOUR
dist.: BBC Television Enterprises Film Sales, Sale; 1979: p.c.: BBC Continuing Education Television. p. Howard Smith. sc. Nicholas Pronay.
Film. 16mm. sd. b&w. 25 min.
Concentrates on the way in which Neville Chamberlain first mastered the techniques of this new medium of mass communication, and then reaped his reward in the way the newsreels covered the Munich crisis of 1938.

ILLUSIONS OF REALITY. PART 3: ONCE A HUN...
dist.: BBC Television Enterprises Film Sales, Sale; 1979: p.c.: BBC Continuing Education Television. p. Howard Smith. sc. Nicholas Pronay.
Film. 16mm. sd. b&w. 25 min.
Examines the way in which the newsreels' view of Hitler's Germany changed.

ILLUSIONS OF REALITY. PART 4: BRITAIN MUST BE STRONG
dist.: BBC Television Enterprises Film Sales, Sale; 1979: p.c.: BBC Continuing Education Television. p. Howard Smith. sc. Nicholas Pronay.
Film. 16mm. sd. b&w. 25 min.
How did the newsreels deal with the important, controversial and very unpopular issue of rearmament?

ILLUSIONS OF REALITY. PART 5: ... WITH A SOCIAL PURPOSE
dist.: BBC Television Enterprises Film Sales, Sale; 1979: p.c.: BBC Continuing Education Television. p. Howard Smith. sc. Nicholas Pronay.
Film. 16mm. sd. b&w. 25 min.
How does the newsreels' picture of social conditions in thirties Britain compare with that given by the much more famous—but less influential—documentaries?

ILLUSIONS OF REALITY. PART 6: WONDERFUL BRITAIN

dist.: BBC Television Enterprises Film Sales, Sale; 1979: p.c.: BBC Continuing Education Television. p. Howard Smith. sc. Nicholas Pronay.
Film. 16mm. sd. b&w. 25 min.
To what extent did the newsreels project and emphasise an image of Britain which coincided with the National Government's approach to the problems of the thirties?

PROPAGANDA WITH FACTS. PART 1: AND, AS FAR AS POSSIBLE, THE WHOLE TRUTH

dist.: BBC Television Enterprises Film Sales, Sale; 1978: p.c.: BBC Continuing Education Television. p. Howard Smith. sc. Nicholas Pronay.
Film. 16mm. sd. b&w. 25 min.
This series examines the value as historical evidence of cinema newsreels, documentaries and television news from the 1930s to the present day. It consists largely of extracts from newsreels and documentaries with some excerpts from feature films of the period. It concentrates on the forties, on the way in which the cinema was used as one of the main instruments of wartime propaganda and how both the ideas and the methods developed during the war were applied to the problems of peace and reconstruction. Programme 1 concentrates on the aims and methods of wartime propaganda, and the longer term effects of both in the early years after the war. Intended audience: General, and for use in the support of media studies in further education colleges.

PROPAGANDA WITH FACTS. PART 2: THAT MALIGNANCY IN OUR MIDST

dist.: BBC Television Enterprises Film Sales, Sale; 1978: p.c.: BBC Continuing Education Television. p. Howard Smith. sc. Nicholas Pronay.
Film. 16mm. sd. b&w. 25 min.
The way in which the public was persuaded to develop an anti-spy, anti-saboteur mentality—to develop attitudes of mind which were in fact just the kind of attitudes we were supposed to be fighting against.

PROPAGANDA WITH FACTS. PART 3: THE NEW JERUSALEM

dist.: BBC Television Enterprises Film Sales, Sale; 1978: p.c.: BBC Continuing Education Television. p. Howard Smith. sc. Nicholas Pronay.
Film. 16mm. sd. b&w. 25 min.
The projection, at home and abroad, of British war aims and the building up of expectations of major social changes—expectations which were to collapse almost immediately after the 1945 election but which were a powerful influence in Labour's overwhelming victory at the polls.

PROPAGANDA WITH FACTS. PART 4: TODAY'S CRISIS . . .

dist.: BBC Television Enterprises Film Sales, Sale; 1978: p.c.: BBC Continuing Education Television. p. Howard Smith. sc. Nicholas Pronay.
Film. 16mm. sd. b&w. 25 min.
The presentation of the almost endless series of crises which fell upon the victorious British people after August 1945, ending with the postponement of many of the changes long planned and expected and their replacement by conscription and re-armament.

PROPAGANDA WITH FACTS. PART 5: OUR SOVIET FRIENDS

dist.: BBC Television Enterprises Film Sales, Sale; 1978: p.c.: BBC Continuing Education Television. p. Howard Smith. sc. Nicholas Pronay.
Film. 16mm. sd. b&w. 25 min.
One of the trickiest propaganda problems of the war was how to change from the anti-communist line of 1939–41 to support for Russia, and later how to placate the sensitive Russians without giving too much ammunition to their supporters in Britain. After 1945, with the development of cold war attitudes, the view of the Soviet Union changed once again.

PROPAGANDA WITH FACTS. PART 6: DON'T TELL 'EM YOU'VE COME TO WIN THE WAR

dist.: BBC Television Enterprises Film Sales, Sale; 1978: p.c.: BBC Continuing Education Television. p. Howard Smith. sc. Nicholas Pronay.
Film. 16mm. sd. b&w. 25 min.
A parallel problem was the necessity for this country to adjust first to the massive scale of the American war effort, and then to the fact that after 1945 we were no longer an equal partner in the alliance.

ABBREVIATIONS

auth.	author
b&w.	black and white
comp.	compiler
dist.	distributor
min.	minutes
mm.	millimetres
p.	producer
p.c.	production company
p.i.	producing institution
sc.	scriptwriter
sd.	sound

DISTRIBUTORS' ADDRESSES

BBC Television Enterprises Film Sales
Woodlands
80 Wood Lane
London W12 0TT
01-734 5588

Higher Education Film & Video Library
c/o Scottish Central Film Library
Dowanhill
74 Victoria Crescent Road
Glasgow G12 9JN
041-334 9314

For *purchase* please apply direct to
BUFVC
55 Greek Street
London W1V 5LR
01-734 3687

Macmillan Education Hirings
25 The Burroughs
Hendon
London NW4 4AT
01-202 7134

For *purchase* please apply direct to
Macmillan Education Ltd
Sales Dept
Houndmills
Basingstoke, Hants
0256 64481

Open University Educational Enterprises Ltd
12 Cofferidge Close
Stony Stratford
Milton Keynes MK11 1BY
0908 566744

Subject Index to Abstracts

(Numbers refer to abstracts)

Abdication crisis, 108, 117

Abyssinia, 76, 80, 83, 103, 278

Advertising, 86

Anstey, Edgar, 165, 211

Army Film and Photographic Unit, 165, (168), (169), (173), (258), (263), 271, 308

Association of Cine-Technicians, 77, 150, 171, 180, 199, 202, 207, 224, 226, 237, 238, 255

Attlee, Clement R., 223

Audiences, 22, 23, 25, 28, 34, 86, 122, 126, 137, 138, 139, 144, 145, 153, 158, 159, 162, 166, 183, 203, 204, 212, 214, 255, 274, 287, 289, 296, 303

BBC, 85, 91, 111, 130, 187, 205, 214, 237, 245, 254, 276

BBC *Television Newsreel*, 205, 206, 208, 212, 237, 245, 257, 259, 261, 304 See *history under section* Documentation Centres—BBC Written Archives Centre

Baldwin, Stanley, 17, 306, 317

Battle of the Somme, The, 3, 140

Bartlett, Vernon, 38

Behr, Louis, 117

Belsen concentration camp, 291, 308

Bernerd, Jeffrey, 62, 122, 127, 128

Bernstein, Sidney L., 212, 213, 214, 219, 220, 222, 224, 233, 234

Bevin, Ernest, 36

Biograph Company, 226

Bishop, H. W., 57, 169

'Blonde Amazon, The', 97, 103, (303)

Boat Race, 16, 245

Boer War, 1, 123, 226

Bracken, Brendan, 185

British Board of Film Censors, 38, 42, 148

British Film Producers Association, 198

British Movietone News, 17, 65, 82, 110, 124, 138, 209, 218, 219, 272, 305, 314

British News, 161

British Paramount News, 22, 28, 39, 50, 61, 80, 98, 110, 119, 120, 122, 126, 138, 148, 157, 165, 207, 280, 293, 294, 297, 300

British Screen News, 13, 15

British Screen Tatler, 14

British Topical Company, 3

Buchenwald concentration camp, 185

CEA *See* Cinema Exhibitors' Association

Cameramen, 9, 11, 12, 59, 62, 64, 76, 89, 93, 124, 130, 140, 141, 142, 143, 151, 156, 165, 168, 169, 173, 176, 190, 191, 192, 193, 207, 226, 229, 258, 263, 267, 268, 271, 273, 295, 308

See also British newsreel companies: Staffing 1910–45

Camerawork, 59, 90, 105, 119, 224

Campbell, Sir Malcolm, 73, 138

Capital and Provincial News Theatres Ltd, (153)

See also under section Newsreel Organisations: The News and Specialised Theatre Association of Great Britain and Northern Ireland

Castleton-Knight, L., 62, 89, 252, 273

Censorship, 23, 35, 38, 39, 41, 43, 49, 71, 101, 111, 112, 117, 123, 132, 143, 144, 148, 149, 150, 153, 154, 155, 156, 157, 164, 169, 195, 197, 270, 278, 293, 294, 297

Central Office of Information, 210, 211, 217, 246

Chamberlain, Neville, 127, 281, 289

Chicago Steel riots, 120

Children; attitudes to newsreels, 137

Children's cinemagazines, 247

China, 122, 125, 126, 127, 210

Churchill, Sir Winston, 215, 223

Cinema Exhibitors' Association, 28, 34, 67, 92, 154, 172, 186, 187, 189, 228, 230, 231, 232, 234, 235, 239, 240, 242, 260, 265

Cinemagazines, 13, 14, 15, 58, 60, 63, 64, 79, 158, 195, 211, 247

See also Children's cinemagazines

Clark, Sir Kenneth, 158

Cold War, 286

Colour, 47, 113, 131, 133, 135, 168, 188, 226, 249, 251, 252, 253, 254, 255, 262

Commentaries, 50, 53, 58, 64, 66, 68, 73, 78, 82, 87, 94, 104, 110, 119, 124, 130, 135, 138, 146, 153, 162, 204, 210, 223, 225, 249, 252, 254, 273, 280, 288, 289, 300, 301, 314

"Commentator, The"; identity, 115

Companies; structure, 2, 64, 65, 76, 79, 89, 98, 118, 130, 247, 274, 287

Conan Doyle, Sir Arthur, 3

Concentration camps, 185, 186, 291

Conservative Party, 209, 215, 216, 218, 311, 316

Content; Newsreels, 13, 15, 17, 21, 22, 30, 31, 35, 36, 37, 43, 56, 58, 63, 64, 78, 95, 96, 117, 126, 127, 128, 129, 139, 147, 183, 188, 197, 204, 213, 214, 223, 227, 255, 259, 262

Coronations, 112, 113, 114, 117, 226, 249, 253, 256

Craig, Sir Gordon, 216, 217
Cuba, 71
Cummings, A. J., 148, 152
Cummins, G. Thomas, 24, 39, 49, 80, 98, 100,
   117, 119, 126, 128, 129, 157, 273
Cup Final, 16, 27, 50, 84, 88, 260
Cutting *See* Editing
Czechoslovakia, 148

Daily Cinema News (?), 93
Delhi Durbar, 226
Dennis, P. W., 144, 145
Dickson, W. K. L., 1, 226
Distribution; Newsreels, 27, 65, 89, 98, 106, 111,
   155, 170, 174, 195, 210, 227, 234, 235, 236, 246,
   249, 253, 274, 280, 287

Eclair Journal, 226, 269
Eden, Sir Anthony, 144, 196
Editing, 62, 90, 115, 119, 124, 130, 248
Editing by exhibitors, 55
Editorial policies, 19, 30, 37, 47, 49, 52, 57, 60,
   63, 78, 87, 90, 100, 105, 110, 111, 119, 139, 182,
   274, 275, 276, 293
Edward, Duke of Windsor, 108, 116, 117
Elvin, George H., 150, 180
Emblems; newsreel companies, 133, 273
Emmett, E. V. H., 110, 138, 288
Empire News Bulletin, 269
Europe in Ferment, 38
Eve's Film Review, 13, 15
Exclusive rights, 20, 41, 49, 50, 52, 70, 88, 89,
   226, 258
Exhibition, 28, 34, 67, 78, 127, 129, 144, 146,
   153, 170, 212, 228, 230, 232, 233, 234, 235, 236,
   245, 255
   See also Cinema Exhibitors' Association

Fascism; Great Britain, 26, 28, 30, 136
Film and Photo League, 298, 309
Film stock; rationing, 170, 174, 178, 184, 188,
   195, 212, 215, 227, 255
   See also Safety film stock
Foreign Office, 38, 311
Franco, Francisco, 142, 146, 288, 302
Free World, The, 176, 179, 197

Gaumont-British News, 89, 110, 112, 115, 138,
   262, 280, 288, 296, 300, 301, 302
Gaumont Graphic, 2, 11, 13, 15, 35, 226
Gaumont Mirror, 13, 15
Germany, 35, 155, 159, 160, 185, 186, 291, 293,
   300, 301, 313
Gordon, Kenneth, 226, 244, 273
Granada Theatres Ltd, 212, 213, 232, 233

Grand National, 41, 62, 70, 227
Grierson, John, 103, 106, 117, 147, 155, 160
Guernica, 115, 302

Harrisson, Tom, 162, 317
Hitler, Adolf, 26, 127
Hore-Belisha, Leslie, 67, 157
Hunger marchers, 22, 23

Inside Nazi Germany, 211
International Brigades, 152, 288
International Review, 232, 233, 246
Interviewing, 16, 140, 146
Ireland (Republic), 195, 244

Jeffrey, R. E., 53, 138, 142, 146

KRS *See* Kinematograph Renters' Society
Kinematograph Renters' Society, 235, 236, 239,
   240, 242

Labour Party, 215, 216, 217, 218, 220
Length; Newsreels, 2, 10, 11, 69, 73, 78, 130, 170,
   178, 188, 206, 213, 227, 238, 249, 250, 254, 255,
   262
Lenses, long-focus, 88, 104, 117
Libraries *See* Newsfilm Libraries
Lloyd George, David, 35, 36
Logos; newsreel companies, 133, 273

Malins, Geoffrey H., 3, 9
Mander, Geoffrey Le, 148, 152
March of Time, 58, 60, 63, 86, 175, 197, 211, 241,
   305
Mass Observation, 162, 317
Matuszewski, Boleslaw, 282
Mergers, 99, 112, 213, 262
Metro News, 208
Military forces, British, 299
Ministry of Information, 158, 161, 167, 168, 175,
   176, 177, 178, 179, 183, 185, 197
Mitchell, Leslie, 138, 300, 314
Mitford, Unity Valkyrie, 157
Monopoly; Newsreel companies, 181, 208, 210,
   219, 222, 224, 246
Monseigneur News Theatre Circuit, (153), 232
   See also under section Newsreel Organisations:
   The News and Specialised Theatre Association
   of Great Britain and Northern Ireland
Montague, W. P., 155
Morrison, Herbert, 26, 218
Mosley, Sir Oswald, 28, 136
Music, 47, 119, 210, 225
Music; copyright, 40
Mussolini, Benito, 80, 83, 127

National News, 118, 121, 130, 131, 133, 134
News and Newsreel, 257, 261, 304
News and Specialised Theatre Association of Great Britain and Northern Ireland, 231
See also under section Newsreel Organisations
News Bulletin, 261, 304
News theatres, 18, 29, 30, 37, 48, 51, 52, 55, 72, 79, 81, 96, 153, 228, 231, 243
News theatres; architecture, 32, 33, 44, 45, 46, 54, 74, 75, 109
News theatres; programmes, 48, 52, 55, 67, 81, 86, 96, 153, 166
Newsfilm libraries, 10, 11, 20, 225, 241, 259, 272, 276, 282, 287
Newspapers; compared with newsreels, 2, 19, 24, 40, 49, 51, 56, 73, 78, 84, 96, 101, 108, 116, 117, 128, 129, 139, 142, 144, 145, 148, 149, 151, 152, 157, 167, 169, 173, 175, 182, (183), 194, 210, 212, 214, 274, 276, 289, 302
Newsreel Association of Great Britain and Ireland, 171, 176, 180, 189, 190, 194, 198, 199, 202, 207, 208, 210, 228, 232, 234, 235, 236, 238, 239, 240, 246
Noble, George, 93
Noble, Ronnie, 258
Northern Ireland, 132
Nuremberg Trials, 196

Official War Office Kinematographers, 4, 9

Palestine, 305
Paris, 39
Pathé Gazette, 50, 79, 110, 140, 226
Pathé News, 204, 212, 305
Pathé Pictorial, 13, 15, 64, 79
Pathé Super Gazette, 12, 13, 15
Pathétone Weekly, 64, 79
'Pinching' *See* Piracy
Piracy, 20, 27, 70, 226, 258, 263, 267, 268
Political aspects, 26, 28, 34, 35, 36, 52, 82, 92, 97, 132, 144, 145, 153, 154, 157, 159, 162, 175, 182, 187, 189, 204, 209, 210, 212, 215, 216, 217, 218, 219, 220, 221, 222, 223, 224, 276, 278, 279, 288, 293, 294, 297, 298, 300, 301, 311, 316
Pooling *See* Rota System
Preservation, 259, 272, 276, 290
Press *See* Newspapers
Production; Newsreels, 2, 11, 12, 16, 19, 27, 29, 59, 61, 64, 65, 68, 69, 76, 84, 89, 98, 107, 113, 119, 124, 197, 200, 201, 206, 224, 225, 227, 238, 241, 247, 274, 275, 280, 287, 303
Propaganda, 34, 35, 36, 52, 72, 92, 97, 101, 103, 123, 132, 139, 143, 147, 150, 155, 158, 164, 165, 183, 188, 194, 217, 276, 278, 279, 288, 293
Radio, 79, 96, 135, 182, (183), 289, 314

Release days; newsreels, 47, 58, 213, 214, 227
Research; methodology, 259, 277, 280, 282, 283, 290, 301, 307, 312
Riots; Chicago, 120
Riots; London, 22, 23, 136
Riots; Paris, 39
Roosevelt, Franklin Delano, 127
Rosenthal, Joseph, 226
Rota System, 114, 115, 167, 168, 175, 176, 197, 207, 208, 213, 238
Royal rota, 113, 114, 115, 208, 229

Safety film stock, 245
Sanger, Gerald F., 23, 41, 55, 68, 82, 87, 116, 117, 124, 149, 164, 182, 194, 218, 219, 254, 300
Scoops, 10, 20, 41, 65, 79, 107, 119, 184
Scripts, 66, 288
Shanghai, 83, 122, 126, 127
Shortt, Edward, 38
Simon, Sir John, 35
Slade Film History Register, 282, 290
See also under section Documentation Centres
Snape, Cecil R., 117, 118, 130
Socialist newsreels, 309, 317
Somme; Battle of, 3, 140
Sound recording, 47, 85, 104, 121, 225, 275
Spanish Civil War, 97, 99, 102, 103, 115, 142, 143, 146, 152, 278, 279, 280, 283, 288, 302, 303
Steed, Wickham, 148, 297
Stockshots *See under* Newsfilm libraries
Stories, 13, 15, 17, 21, 22, 23, 31, 39, 43, 47, 57, 61, 71, 73, 90, 95, 97, 100, 102, 111, 114, 115, 120, 122, 125, 126, 127, 128, 129, 130, 136, 148, 157, 160, 165, 185, 186, 204, 206, 210, 214, 262, 280, 288, 291, 292, 293, 294, 297, 300, 302
Strikes, 115, 116, 120, 209

Telenews, 208, 209, 232
Television, 54, 56, 85, 91, 111, 151, 184, 188, 204, 205, 206, 207, 208, 212, 213, 214, 227, 238, 243, 245, 247, 251, 254, 255, 260, 261, 264, 266, 268, 272, 287, 291, 292
See also BBC and BBC *Television Newsreel*
This Modern Age, 211, 241
Thomas, Howard, 214, 227, 251
3-D newsreels, 250, 251
Topical Budget, 4, 5, 6, 7, 8, 226, 269, 315
'Topical' films, 1, 2, 10, 42, 107, 163, 226, 269, 284, 287
See also Appendix 2

Universal Talking News, 50, 106, 110, 112, 122, 125, 138, 262, 280

Visnews, 292

War Office, 3, 6, 7, 9, 140, 156, 165
War Office Cinematograph Committee, 4, 5, 226, 315
War Pictorial News, 168
Warwick Chronicle, 226, 269
Watts, Fred, 69, 91, 184
Welt im Film, 313
Williamson's Animated News, 226

Windsor, Edward, Duke of, 108, 116, 117
Women; attitudes to newsreels, 25
Woodroffe, Thomas, 130, 135
Workers' Newsreel, 298, 309
Workers' Topical News, 298, 309
World in Action (Canada), 211
World War 1; 3, 9, 140, 287
World War 2; 203, 287, 293, 294, 310, 317
Wyand, Paul, 263